Islamic Art

in Iranian Painting

Nadir Mohammed Shalbi

Content

1. Introduction 01-42

2. Iranian Painting 43-59

3. Islamic Art in Iran 60-93

4. Main Schools of Iranian Painting 94-138

5. Concluding Remarks 139-169

CHAPTER I

INTRODUCTION

(A) What is Islam?
(B) What is Islamic Art?
(C) The Relation Between Islamic Art and Islamic World-View

CHAPTER I

INTRODUCTION

Before describing the Islamic Art and its forms it seems desirable to discuss briefly what 'Islam' is?

(A) WHAT IS ISLAM?

By ***'Islam'*** we mean the religion preached by the Prophet of Islam - Muḥammad - in the A.D. 600s. Muḥammad was an Arab who was born in Mecca about 570. He was a son of the noble parents – 'Abdullah and Āaminah. He believed he had been sent by Allah to warn and guide his people and to call them to worship only One God *(Allah)*. Muḥammad, preached that there is only One God and that he (Muhammad) was God's messenger. Those who believe in the One God and accept Muḥammad as His messenger are called 'Muslim's. The word "Muslim" is an Arabic word that means 'One who submits to God (Allah). 'Islam' is an Arabic term equivalent to "submission".[1] The Western scholars often call Islam as 'Muḥammadanism' and its followers 'Muḥamamdans', which is incorrect, because Muslims feel that these terms (Muḥammadanism and Muḥamadans) give the wrong impression that Muslims worship Muḥammad. But, in reality Muslims believe in *Tawḥīd* (Unity of God) and they do not worship anything except *'Allah'*.

Islam is not derived after the name of any particular religious personality like other religions. The very term **'Islam'** has been used by Allah in the Qur'ān and that is why this world-view is named **'Islam'**. The stipulation is distinctively recommended by Allah and therefore any name insinuating any relation with any human being is categorically unacceptable to Muslims as the Qur'ān says:

إِنَّ الدِّينَ عِندَ اللهِ الإِسلاَمُ

The Religion before God is Islam (submission to

His Will): (Surah III: Āl-i-Imrān:19)

The word **'Islam'** does not merely mean 'submission' but has a vast connotation. Justice Amīr 'Alī has very lucidly explained the concept of Islam in his *The Spirit of Islam* as under :

> The religion of Jesus bears the name of Christianity, derived from his designation of Christ; that of Moses and of Buddha are known by the respective names of their teachers. The religion of Mohammed alone has a distinctive appellation. It is Islam.
>
> In order to form a just appreciation of the religion of Mohammed it is necessary to understand aright the true significance of the word Islam. *Salam (salama)*, in its primary sense, means, to be tranquil, at rest, to have done one's duty, to have paid up, to be at perfect peace; in its secondary sense, to surrender oneself to Him with whom peace is made. The noun derived from it means peace, greeting, safety, salvation. The word does not imply, as is commonly supposed absolute submission to God's will, but means, on the contrary, striving after righteousness.[2]

Islam is one of the world's largest religions and the largest Muslim communities exist in the Middle East, North Africà, Indonesia, Bangladesh. Pakistan, India and the Central Asian Republics. In Europe, Islam is the principal religion in European Turkey and Albania. The once great Muslim empires no longer exist. But Muslims are still united by their faith, which forms a common bond of culture among them. This peculair unity is based upon the significant teachings of Islam, because according to the Holy Qur'ān:

إِنَّمَا الْمُؤْمِنُونَ إِخْوَةٌ.

"The Believers are but a single Brotherhood".

In the following pages we shall briefly discuss the main teachings of Islam in order to understand its true spirit as a universal religion.

MAIN TEACHINGS OF ISLAM :

The companions of Prophet Muḥammad preserved the revelations that came to Muḥammad by memorizing them or writing them down. Muslim scholars believe Muḥammad approved there teachings. Later the materials were combined to form the Holy Book of the Muslims. It is called the Qur'ān, from the Arabic word ('قرت') meaning 'recitation'. Muslims consider the Qur'ān to the word of God Himself, spoken to Muḥammad by an angel named Gabriel. The Holy Book calls this angel : *Ruḥ-ul-āmīn* (the spirit of Faith and Truth) the epithet of Gabriel, who came with the inspired Messages to the Holy Prophet. Thus the Qur'ān says :

وَإِنَّهُ لَتَنْزِيلُ رَبِّ الْعَالَمِينَ. نَزَلَ بِهِ الرُّوحُ الأَمِينُ

"Verily this is a Revelation from the lord of the worlds : with it came down the spirit of Faith and Truth".[4]

Parts of the Holy Book resemble the Bible, the Apocrypha and the Talmad. The Qur'ān contains many stories about the prophets that have already appeared in the old Testament. The Qur'ān also had stories from the new Testament about Jesus, whom it calls the word of God.

The Holy Book provides the guide-line for its believers. The Muslim faith is based upon the five principles. These are also called the pillars of Islam:-

1) Unity of God (*al-Tawḥīd*) 'التوحيد'
2) Divine Justice (*'adl-i-Ilhaī*) 'العدل الٰهی'
3) Prophethood (*al-Nubuwwah*) 'النبوت'
4) Imamah 'الامامت'
5) Day of Resurrection (al-ma'ād). 'المعاد'

The above five principle are accepted by shi'ites. Of these only three are believed to be the principles of faith by Sunnis : 1) Unity of God; 2) Prophethood; and 3) Ma'ād.

Some main **teachings of Islam** are as follows :

(a) God and Humanity :

The Qur'ān teaches the Absolute Unity and power of God, the Creator of the whole Universe. The Unity of God, His immateriality, His Majesty, His Mercy, His creativity form the constant and never-ending theme of the Holy Book. The following verses of the Chapter II of the Qur'ān most eloquently explain about **Allah** :

وَإِلٰهُكُمْ إِلٰهٌ وَاحِدٌ لَا إِلٰهَ إِلَّا هُوَ الرَّحْمٰنُ الرَّحِيمُ. إِنَّ فِي خَلْقِ السَّمٰوَاتِ وَالْأَرْضِ وَاخْتِلَافِ اللَّيْلِ
وَالنَّهَارِ وَالْفُلْكِ الَّتِي تَجْرِي فِي الْبَحْرِ بِمَا يَنْفَعُ النَّاسَ وَمَا أَنْزَلَ اللّٰهُ مِنَ السَّمَاءِ مِنْ مَاءٍ فَأَحْيَا
بِهِ الْأَرْضَ بَعْدَ مَوْتِهَا وَبَثَّ فِيهَا مِنْ كُلِّ دَابَّةٍ وَتَصْرِيفِ الرِّيَاحِ وَالسَّحَابِ الْمُسَخَّرِ بَيْنَ السَّمَاءِ
وَالْأَرْضِ لَآيَاتٍ لِقَوْمٍ يَعْقِلُونَ.

"And your God
Is One God :
There is no god
But He,
Most Gracious,
Most Merciful"

Behold! In the creation
Of the heavens and the earth;
In the alternation
Of the Night and the Day;
In the sailing of the ships
Through the Ocean
For the profit of mankind;
In the rain which God
Sends down from the skies,
And the life which He gives therewith
To an earth that is dead;
In the beasts of all kinds
That He scatters
Through the earth;
In the change of the winds,
And the clouds which they
Trial like their slaves
Between the sky and the earth;
(Here) indeed are signs
For a people that are wise.[5]

The Qur'ān also teaches that God is the Just, Gracious and Merciful, and wishes people to repent and purify themselves so that they can attain to the Blessings of Allah in the life and in lifehare-after. Therefore, God sends prophets with sacred books to teach people their duty to God and humanity. The Muslims believe that Prophet Muḥammed was the last of the prophets: "Muḥammad is the Apostle of God, and the seal of the Prophets"[6] Jesus and the old Testament prophets were his predecessors : "And who believe in the Revelation sent to thee, and sent before they time..."[7]

The Qur'ān forbids the representation of human and animal figures (especially represented for worship). In view of the same the orthodox Islamic art rarely pictures living beings. The Qur'ān also denounces usury, games of chance, and the consumption of pork and alcohal.[8] According to the Qur'ān the righteousness comes from a secure faith, from sincere devotion to God and from unselfish service to humanity.[9]

(b) Ethical Ideal :

Ethics, like other Islamic sciences, takes its origin from the Holy Qur'ān. In one word, it can he said that ethics or moral philosophy is wholly based on it. The Qur'ān lays down the foundation of a religious system on purely ethical principles, hence there is not much to distinguish between Islam as such and Islamic ethics.[10]

The following verses of the Holy Qur'ān clearly explain the notion of Ethics : وَاعْبُدُوا اللّٰهَ وَلَا تُشْرِكُوا بِهٖ شَيْئًا وَّبِالْوَالِدَيْنِ اِحْسَانًا وَّبِذِى الْقُرْبٰى وَالْيَتٰمٰى وَالْمَسٰكِيْنِ وَالْجَارِ ذِى الْقُرْبٰى وَالْجَارِ الْجُنُبِ وَالصَّاحِبِ بِالْجَنْۢبِ وَابْنِ السَّبِيْلِ وَمَا مَلَكَتْ اَيْمَانُكُمْ

Serve God, and join not
Any partners with Him;
And do good —
To parents, kins folk,
Orphans, those in need,

Neighbours who are near,
Nighbours who are stranger,
The Companion by your side,
The way-farer [ye meet],
And what your right hands possess:[11]

وَالَّذِيْنَ إِذَا أَنْفَقُوا لَمْ يُسْرِفُوا وَلَمْ يَقْتُرُوا وَكَانَ بَيْنَ ذٰلِكَ قَوَاماً

Those who, when they spend,
Are not extravagant and not
Niggardly, but hold a just (balance)
Between those (extremes);[12]

إِنَّ اللّٰهَ يَامُرُ بِالعَدْلِ وَالإِحْسَانِ وَإِيْتَاءِ ذِي الْقُرْبٰى وَيَنْهٰى عَنِ الْفَحْشَاءِ
وَالْمُنْكَرِ وَالْبَغْيِ يَعِظُكُمْ لَعَلَّكُمْ تَذَكَّرُوْنَ

God commands justice, the doing
Of good, and liberality to kith
And kin, and He forbids
All shameful deeds, and injustice
And rebellion: He instructs you,
That ye may receive admonition.[13]

اَلَّذِيْنَ يُنْفِقُوْنَ فِي السَّرَّاءِ وَالضَّرَّاءِ وَالْكٰظِمِيْنَ الْغَيْظَ وَالْعَافِيْنَ عَنِ
النَّاسِ وَاللّٰهُ يُحِبُّ الْمُحْسِنِيْنَ

Those who spend (freely),
Whether in prosperity,
Or in adversity;
Who restrain anger,
And pardon(all) men;
For God loves those
Who do good;[14]

يَاأَيُّهَا النَّاسُ إِنَّا خَلَقْنٰكُمْ مِنْ ذَكَرٍ وَأُنْثٰى وَجَعَلْنٰكُمْ شُعُوْبًا وَقَبَائِلَ لِتَعَارَفُوْا إِنَّ أَكْرَمَكُمْ
عِنْدَ اللّٰهِ أَتْقٰكُمْ إِنَّ اللّٰهَ عَلِيْمٌ خَبِيْرٌ

O mankind! We created
You from a single (pair)
Of a male and female,

And made you into
Nations and tribes, that
Ye may know each other
[Not that ye may despair
[Each other]. Verily
The most honoured of you
In the sight of God
Is (he who is) the most
Righteous of you.
And God has full knowledge
And is well acquainted
[With all things].[15]

The sacred Book is full of such injunctions which high-light that ethical principles are the secret essence of Islam. Kindness to parents,[16] forgiveness to those who err,[17] piety,[18] equity, just dealing,[19] Compassion,[20] restraint of lust,[21] true nobility, modesty etc., all find proper mention in the Holy Qur'ān.

Prof. M.Ummaruddin explains that morality in Islam is nothing but the system of injunctions laid down by the Holy Book. He refers to the Holy Prophet as the ethical ideal for the Muslims. Referring to Al-Ghazzālī he points out that the life of Muḥammad was the life of an ideally perfect man :

> Ethics in Islam is nothing but the body of injunctions laid down in the Qur'ān for the practical conduct of life and fully exemplified in the practice of the Holy Prophet throughout his life. The Qur'ān addresses the Prophet, "Thou has been created within excellent character". The Prophet himself says, "I have been sent to perfect morals". Some one asked the Prophet, "What is religion?" "Good character" was the reply. Al-Ghazzālī considered the Prophet as the ideally perfect man, par excellence, in all aspects of life. The Qur'ān exhorts the believers to follow the rightly guided, particularly the Prophet. "It is the desire of every pious Muslim to model his life in every possible particular upon that of the Prophet".[22]

Further, the Qur'ān, like the Bible, forbids lying, stealing, adultery and dishonesty. Punishment for some offenses, such as theft, adultery and murder, can be severe. But the Qur'ān softened the ancient law of "an eye for an eye, a tooth for a tooth" by permitting the payment of "blood money" and by urging forgiveness. Islam has much regard for those who leave the virtue of forgiveness :

فَأُولَٰئِكَ عَسَىٰ اللَّهُ أَنْ يَعْفُوَ عَنْهُمْ وَكَانَ اللَّهُ عَفُوًّا غَفُورًا .

For these, there is hope
That God will forgive :
For God doth blot out (sins)
And forgive again and again.[23]

خُذِ الْعَفْوَ وَأْمُرْ بِالْعُرْفِ وَأَعْرِضْ عَنِ الْجَاهِلِينَ

Hold to forgiveness :
Command what is right;
But turn away from the ignorant.[24]

The Qur'ān permits slavery under certain conditions, but urges that slaves be freed. It permits a man to have as many as four wives under certain condition.[25] The Holy Book, in it true sense, is a book of moral principles. "It is a book which emplasizes 'deed' rather than 'idea'."[26]

(c) Virtue and Justice :

As mentioned earlier, the Qur'ān teaches to show honor to parents, kindness to slaves, protection for orphans and widows, and charity to the poor. It teaches the virtues of faith in Oneness of God, kindness, honesty, industry, honor. courage. loyality and generosity. It condemns mistrust, impatience, and cruelty and all vicious actions. Heads of families must treat household members kindly and fairly. A wife has rights against her husband to protect her from abuse.

The Holy Book teaches that a person should not refuse requests for help even if they seem unnecessary. God judges the dishonest petitioner and rewards the giver in this and the next world.

According to the Qur'ān in order to achieve the moral end or Ideal one has to build a good character which comprises of all the virtues, the most important of which is the love of God. Virtues and justice lead a man nearer to God — Who is the main goal of human life. M. Umaruddin explain Virtues and Vices referring to Al-Ghazzālī's view point that the inter-action of intellect, self-assertation and appetition produces virtues and vices. He says that if the above three faculties are used in right direction, they produce virtues and if they follow on the wrong lines, vices are bound to result.[27]

Justice (*'Adl*) according to the Holy Scripture is the virtue of keeping to the golden mean between the extremes of knowledge [*Ḥikmat*] appetition [in right-sense '*Iffah*' [chastify or temperance] and self-assertation [courage or *Shaja'a* and not in wrong sense *Shahwa* or cowardice *Jubn*] and of maintain the balance between them. Justice requires that one should fulfil one's duties and no one should go beyond the prescribed limits. Everything should be put in its proper place. Moreover, justice has vast connotation in Islam and in real sense it is the sole criterion of reward and punishment and intimate source of true and faithful relationship among human beings and between man and God. The following verses of the Holy Qur'ān clearly explain the notion of justice

إِنَّ اللَّهَ يَأْمُرُ بِالْعَدْلِ وَالْإِحْسَانِ وَإِيتَاءِ ذِي الْقُرْبَىٰ وَيَنْهَىٰ عَنِ الْفَحْشَاءِ
وَالْمُنكَرِ وَالْبَغْيِ يَعِظُكُمْ لَعَلَّكُمْ تَذَكَّرُونَ

God commands justice, the doing
Of good, and liberality to kith
And kin, and He forbids
All shameful deeds, and injustice
And rebellion: He instructs you,
That ye many receive admonition.[28]

فَإِنْ طَائِفَتَانِ مِنَ الْمُؤْمِنِينَ اقْتَتَلُوا فَأَصْلِحُوا بَيْنَهُمَا فَإِنْ بَغَتْ إِحْدَاهُمَا عَلَى الْأُخْرَىٰ فَقَاتِلُوا الَّتِي تَبْغِي
حَتَّىٰ تَفِيءَ إِلَىٰ أَمْرِ اللَّهِ فَإِنْ فَاءَتْ فَأَصْلِحُوا بَيْنَهُمَا بِالْعَدْلِ وَأَقْسِطُوا إِنَّ اللَّهَ يُحِبُّ الْمُقْسِطِينَ .

If two parties among
The Believers fall into
A quarrel, make ye peace
Between them: but if
One of them transgresses
Beyond bounds against the other,
Then fight ye (all) against
The one that transgresses
Until it complies with
The command of God;
But if it complies, them
Make peace between them
With justice, and be fair:
For God loves those
Who are fair (and just).[29]

شَهِدَ اللَّهُ أَنَّهُ لَا إِلَٰهَ إِلَّا هُوَ وَالْمَلَائِكَةُ وَأُولُو الْعِلْمِ قَائِمًا بِالْقِسْطِ لَا إِلَٰهَ إِلَّا هُوَ الْعَزِيزُ الْحَكِيمُ

There is no god but He:
That is the witness of God.
His angels. and those endowed
With knowledge, standing firm
On justice. There is no god but He,
The Exalted in Power,
The Wise....[30]

يَا أَيُّهَا الَّذِينَ آمَنُوا كُونُوا قَوَّامِينَ بِالْقِسْطِ شُهَدَاءَ لِلَّهِ وَلَوْ عَلَىٰ أَنفُسِكُمْ أَوِ الْوَالِدَيْنِ وَالْأَقْرَبِينَ

O believers, be you securers of justice,
witnesses for God, even though it be
against yourselves, or your parents
and kinsmen....[31]

يَادَاوُدُ إِنَّاجَعَلْنَاكَ خَلِيفَةً فِي ٱلأَرْضِ فَاحْكُمْ بَيْنَ ٱلنَّاسِ بِالْحَقِّ وَلاَ تَتَّبِعِ الْهَوَىٰ

David, behold, We have appointed
The a Viceroy in the earth;
Therefore judge between men justly.[32]

(d) *Life and Death :*

Islam teaches that life on earth is a period of testing and preparation for life to come. According to the Qur'ān the terms of 'life' and 'death' at any point of time is to test man and to keep a'check on him: "God who created death and life, that He may try which of you is best in deed: And God is the Exalted in might, of Forgiving"[33]

According to the Holy Qur'ān the creation of man is not mere sport or without a purpose. We do not know the state before our present life or the state after which we can scarcely understand but our present life is clearly given to enable us to perform good deeds to reach a nobler state.

Another important aspect of life and death according to Islam is that those persons who sacrifice their lives and whatever dearest they have in the Way of Allah they are not dead. According to the Qur'ān the Martyrs are not dead: they live, — and for a higher reason and in a deeper sense than in the life they have left. Their real life is sustained from the ineffable Presence and Nearness of God, as the following Qur'ānic Verses unambiguously indicate :

وَلَا تَحْسَبَنَّ الَّذِينَ قُتِلُوا فِي سَبِيلِ اللَّهِ أَمْوَاتًا بَلْ أَحْيَاءٌ عِنْدَ رَبِّهِمْ يُرْزَقُونَ

Think not those
Who are slain in God's way
As dead. Nay, they live,
Finding their sustenance
In the Presence of their Lord:[34]

وَلَا تَقُولُوا لِمَنْ يُقْتَلُ فِي سَبِيلِ اللَّهِ أَمْوَاتٌ بَلْ أَحْيَاءٌ وَلَٰكِنْ لَا تَشْعُرُونَ

And say not of those
Who are slain in the way
Of God: "They are dead."
Nay, they are living
Though ye perceive (it) not.[35]

It is believed that the angels in heaven record a person's good and bad deeds. People should therefore, try their best to be good and help others, and then trust in God's justice and mercy for their reward. In reality death is not the end of life but it is the gate of eternal life.

Muslims believe in the day of judgment when everyone will receive the record of his or her deeds on earth. The record book is placed in the right hand of the good (man), who then go to heaven. It is placed in the left hand of the wicked, who go to hell. The sorrows and tortures of hell resemble those described in the Bible. For Muslim's, heaven is a garden with flowing steams, luxcious fruits, richly covered couches, and beautiful maidens.

Thus, these are the main teachings of Islam. If we discuss them one by one books can be written, but for the present purpose it is sufficient to conclude with the translation of the Chapter II, Verse 1 to 6 of the Holy Qur`ān to present the essence of the ethical principles involved and embodied in Islam:

الٓمٓ ذٰلِكَ ٱلْكِتَابُ لَا رَيْبَ فِيهِ هُدًى لِّلْمُتَّقِينَ .ٱلَّذِينَ يُؤْمِنُونَ بِالْغَيْبِ وَيُقِيمُونَ الصَّلٰوٰةَ
وَمِمَّا رَزَقْنٰهُمْ يُنفِقُونَ وَٱلَّذِينَ يُؤْمِنُونَ بِمَا أُنزِلَ إِلَيْكَ وَمَا أُنزِلَ مِن قَبْلِكَ وَبِالْآخِرَةِ هُمْ يُوقِنُونَ.
أُولٰٓئِكَ عَلٰى هُدًى مِن رَّبِّهِمْ وَأُولٰٓئِكَ هُمُ ٱلْمُفْلِحُونَ

> There is no doubt in this book a guidance to the pious, who believe in the Unseen, who observe the prayers, and distribute (charity) out of what We have bestowed on them; and who believe in that which we have commissioned the with, and in that We commissioned others with before thee, and who have assurance in the life to come;—these have received the direction of their Lord.[36]

In short, the main teachings on the basis of which the Islamic system is know can briefly be summarised in the following words of Syed Amīr 'Alī:

> The principal bases on which the Islamic system is founded are (1) a belief in the unity, immateriality, power, mercy, and supreme love of the Creator; (2) charity and botherhood among mankind; (3) subjugation of the passions; (4) the outpouring of a grateful heart to the Giver of all good; and (5) accountability for human actions in another existence. The grand and noble conceptions expressed in the Qur'ān of the power and love of the Deity surpass everything of their kind in any other language. The unity of God, His Immateriality, His majesty, His mercy, form the constant and neverending theme of the most eloquent and soul-stirring passages. The flow of life, light, and spirituality never ceases. But throughout there is no trace of dogmatism. Appeal is made to the inner consciousness of man, to his intuitive reason alone.[37]

Now we shall discuss Islamic Art in detail in order to understand it in its proper perspective.

(B) WHAT IS ISLAMIC ART?

Generally speaking, Islamic art is the art of the civillization based on the Islamic religion. As stated earlier, the Prophet Muḥammad first preached Islam in Arabia during the early A.D. 600's. The people who follow the teachings of Islam call themselves Muslims. Islam has vast counotalism with regard to every aspect of human life. It defines clearly the purpose of universe and the relationship among the Creator—God, man and universe. The intellectual, Social and aesthetical features of Islamic religion make it distinct from other relations :

> The word "Islamic", as applied to art, refers to those people who have grown and lived under rulers who professed the faith of Islam or in cultures and societies which have been strongly influenced by the modes of life and thought characteristic of Islam. But 'Islamic', unlike 'Christian', refers not only to a faith but also to a whole culture, since — at least in theory — the separation of the realm of Caesar from that of God is not applicable to Islam. Also unlike Christianity, Islam did not develop first as the faith of a few, increasing the numbers of its adherents under the shadow of a huge state alien to it, slowly developing the intellectual and artistic features which were going to characterize it, and, after several centuries, blossoming into an empire and giving birth to an art as well as a philosophy and a social doctrine.[38] .

Arab Muslims began a series of conquests in the A.D. 600's, and united all the countries they conquered into a single civilization (*Ummah*). The Arabs themselves had little art. But through their conquests, they came into contact with the highly developed arts of Persia (now Iran) Syria, Egypt, and Mesopotamia (now Iraq). Generally, it is said that the peoples who accepted

Islam blended their cultural styles and developed a distinct and fairly uniform style of art known as 'Islamic art'. It was the product of many countries, extending from Spain to India. In Spain, Islamic art is called Moorish, from the Muslim group that first inhabited that country in the 700's. From the 900's on, local variations in the art start appearing, but the over-all interrclationship remains intact.

However, there are very powerful yet authentic views on the emergence and evolution of Islamic art. They maintain that Islamic art emerged simultaneously with the very rise of Islam itself :

> Islamic art did not slowly evolve from the meeting of a new faith and of a new state with whatever older traditions prevailed in the areas in which the state ruled; it came forth as suddenly as the faith and the state, for whatever influences may have been at work in the building and decoration of early Islamic monuments, their characteristic is that they were built for Muslims, to serve purposes which did not exist in quite the same way before Islam.[39]

It is essential to refer to same verses of the Qur'ān and few Traditions of the Prophet which clearly endorse the view that Islamic art is inherent in Islam itself:

إِنَّا زَيَّنَّا ٱلسَّمَآءَ الدُّنْيَا بِزِينَةٍ الْكَوَاكِبِ ·

We have indeed decked
The lower heaven with beauty
(In) the stars'—[40]

وَلَقَدْ جَعَلْنَا فِى ٱلسَّمَآءِ بُرُوجًا وَزَيَّنَّٰهَا لِلنَّٰظِرِينَ

It is We Who have set out

The Zodiacal Signs in the heavens,
And made them fair-seeming
To (all) beholders;[41]

In addition to the above Qur'anic Verses a couple of Traditions of the Prophet would be in order : أنَّ اللهَ يُحِبُّ إذَا عَمِلَ أحَدُكُمْ عَمَلاً أنْ يُحْسِنَهُ (كنزالعمال)

"God likes that whenever anyone of you performs any work he should do it in a beautiful manner".[42]

اللهُ جَمِيْلٌ وَيُحِبُّ اَلْجَمَالَ

"God is Beautiful and Likes Beauty".[43]

Highlighting the characteristic of a fine calligraphy Imām 'Alī bin Abī Ṭalib says :

"The beauty of writing is the tongue of the hand and the elegance of thought.[44]

Islamic Art flourished between 800 A.D. and 1700 A.D. and then declined, especially beginning in the later 1700's. It has its own distinctive features and cultural heritage.

The Islamic artists and aestheticians tried at their level best to create and develop various art-forms such as **poetry, music, painting, architecture, book-illustration** and **book-illumination**, **ceramics** and other **minor plastic** and **decorative arts**. They have been deeply inspired by their religions world-view and cultural out-look in this regards :

Islamic artists were most inventive in architecture, especially in *mosques*, their houses of worship, and in palaces and such socially useful institutions as shopping areas and hospitals. They

> also produced beautiful textiles, metalware, pottery, carved and molded plaster, glassware, wood and ivory carings and *book illuminations* (decorations) and buildings. The best of these works show extraordinary mastery of technique, design, and colour. They illustrate a consistent concern to beautify all aspects of daily life.[45]

Moreover, Islamic art includes many beautiful religions colleges called *madrasahs*. Coloured tiles decorate the towers called *minarets*. In reality Islamic art as rightly remarked by Sayyed Hossein Nasr, is the result of Islamic metaphysics and theology which emphasize that God is the origin or source of all forms. He is Omniscient—the Knower of all things and therefore, the essences or forms of all things have their reality in the Divine Intellect.[46]

In the following pages we shall briefly discuss some main characteristics of Islamic art with reference to few of its important forms to understand the secret message and true spirit of this art.

MAIN CHARACTERISTICS OF ISLAMIC ART :

Islam has its specific characteristics. It is considered as a strict religion. There has been a controversy over the issue as to whether or not painting was prohibited by the Prophet of Islam. Some theologians (*ʿUlemas*) prohibited artists from making images of living things. It is said that these*ʿUlemas* feared that people might regard statues or paintings as something 'Divine' that had to be worshiped, rather than as images of God or of saintly figures. Muslims also believed that *Allah* (Arabic word for God) was the One and only Creator of like. They regarded any attempt to paint or form something life-like as trespassing on Allah's position as sole Creator. According to strict Islamic theologians, the artist who made works of art depicting living things was condemned to hell-fire. Muslims usually followed the Islamic laws about images in their religious and public life but they did not always obey these laws so strictly in their private quarters especially between 700 (A.D.) and 1300 (A.D.) and even during later periods especially in India and Iran. The prohibition of pictures was more strictly followed in Turkey and the Arab world—Egypt, Iraq, Syria, and North Africa—than in India or Iran.[47] All the creative artists of Indian sub-continent and Iran did not consider that making images of 'living things' as un-Islamic, but they wanted to highlight the inner creative urges of man; the Vicegerent of God, the co-worker with Him; because Allah has given him power and freedom to create. In order to understand fully the main characteristics of **Islamic art** we shall brief discuss some of its **main forms** :

SOME MAIN FORMS OF ISLAMIC ART :

In this section we shall briefly deal with some of the significant forms of Islamic art in order to assess its unique importance in the history of aesthetics.

(a) Islamic Design Motifs :

This false conception of the prohibition of life-like images channeled Islamic art into different directions. Artists usually avoided the realistic portrayal of human beings and animals. In paintings and reliefs, they designed highly stylized people, animals, and birds. These works have an abstract, flat character that makes them more like symbols than lifelike pictures. Islamic art here was simply a symbolic representation. On the whole, designers preferred floral motifs, but drew even these in an abstract style. Generally these artists developed a special type of decoration consisting of winding stems with abstract leaves. This scrollwork, called *arabesque*, (meaning a design with intertwined leaves or geometrical figures) become common in Islamic art in all Muslim countries beginning in the 900's. Geometric patterning of remarkable sophistication developed in Iraq and Iran in the 1000's and then spread elsewhere as geometry acquired an almost mystical significance in Islamic art.[48]

Briefly, we can say that geometry becomes highly important in Islamic world as its figures and constructions were permeated with symbolic, cosmological and even philosophical significance.[49] We shall thoroughly discuss the Islamic design motif in the Fourth Chapter of this thesis.

(b) Calligraphy :

Another characteristic feature of Islamic art is the wide use of Arabic script, which lends itself to *calligraphy*, the art of beautiful writing. Arabic, which is written from right to left, is the most widely used language in the Middle East. Its script was adopted for Persian, Turkish, Urdu, and most other languages used by Muslims. The Islamic Holy Book, called the *Qur'ān* and non-religious writings often appear on the walls of religious buildings and on art objects. These writings, in various styles, are beautifully executed. Sometimes they are combined with floral or geometric designs, but only rarely with animal or human figures.

It is rightly said that the Qur'ān is the link between the Arabic script and the Islamic world. It is regarded not as the written account of the prophets teachings, but as the very Word of *Allah*. Thus the writing used to record the Words of the Divinity, by its very use assumes a position of great importance in the world of Islam. With this stimulus, it became necessary to use the finest calligraphy that could be achieved using the primitive script the calligraphy is the most significant from in Islamic Art forms. "The word of God together with the hand of man combined to create perhaps the greatest examples of calligraphy in the history of mankind."[50]

Common styles of Arabic calligraphy include *Kufic* and *Neskhi*. Kufic, the formal and angular style of the two, received its name from the city of *Kufah*, Iraq, where this type of writing developed. Islamic scholars used *kufic* for inscriptions until the 1100's. They used it for copying the Qur'ān from the late 600's to about 1000. *Neskhi* was a flowing script that was sometimes set against a background of arabesque designs. Beginning in the 1100's, *Neskhi* calligraphy was increasingly used for writing the Qur'ān.[51] *Kufic* script was reserved for chapter headings. Other, more elaborate, writing styles developed especially in Iran and Turkey and were also used for literature. In short, under Islam, artists were stimulated to excel themselves in all forms of art, employing their mastery and displaying their artistry in beautifying the discourse of God. (See Plate **20** , **30**).

(c) Architecture :

The architecture is considered as the most important feature of Islamic Art. Broadly speaking, we can say that architecture is the hall-mark of Islamic Art. Despite its wide radiation in both time and place, Muslim architecture owed its remarkable unity to a religious faith and an unchanging way of life.

(i) <u>Mosques</u> :

Mosque or *Masjid* literally means a place of 'prostration', a house of worship. Mosques are the main religious buildings of Islam and are usually the most important structures in a Muslim city, village or town. In plan every Mosque or *Masjid* is based on that of Mecca, but Islamic culture enriched itself by contacts with the older cultures of the Middle East.[52] The essential features of a typical mosque include, a courtyard, where worshipers gather; a *mihrab* a gate, and *minarets*. The *miḥrāb* is a small central niche or arched unit that marks the wall nearest to Mecca, which the worshipers must face during prayer. The gate is a monumental, highly decorated structure set into a usually plain *facade* (from facing the street). Minarets are slender, tall towers of various shapes. The faithful are called to prayer *five* times a day from a balcony at the top of a minaret. Inside very mosque is a pulpit called a *mimbar*.[53] Generally, the *mimbar* may be made of wood or stone. Mosque has a significant religio-ethical as well as socio-political importance in the life of a Muslim.

There are some architectural differences amongst the religious structures. Styles of mosques vary from one country to the other. A large dome became the chief feature of the mosques of Persia, India, Turkey and other Arabian countries. A high, arched entrance with a minaret on each side also characterized mosques in Persia and India. The typical Turkish mosque has an enormous enclosed central space covered by a dome and half domes resembling Byzantine churches. The Mosque of Sultan Salim in Ederne Turkey, is a good example of this type. Many Persian, Spanish, and North African mosques are covered with tile-work. In short, the 'Mosque' is, in reality the main religious structure in the Islamic architecture. It has a spiritual significance in the lives of Muslims.

(ii) Madrasahs :

Islam lays much emphasis on *'ilm* (knowledge) and considers it light of the path as well as the destination. So the educational institutions (*Madrasahs*) have been given much importance, say, second only to Mosques. *Madrasahs* or religious colleges also provide important examples of Islamic architecture. The *madrasah* is usually a four-sided building standing around an open courtyard. The centre of each side of the quadrangle consists of an arched large hall, called an *iwan* ('ایوان') which is open to courtyard and used for lectures. Students attend classes in the *iwans* and live in cells that are located along the four sides of the courtyard between the *iwan*. Though it is not compulsory yet they wear a specific type of dress during their class-time and prayers.

(iii) Other Important Buildings :

There are some other sacred buildings which have a spiritual significance in Islamic art. These structures include *Imambaras*, tombs over the graves of *Walis* or *Sufis* which are called *Zeyarts* and *Eid-gahs* and so on. Generally, tombs provide some of the most striking examples of Islamic architecture. Builders cover a tomb with a square or eight-sided building. A dome is built over the building. They also build a round or many sided tower with a roof that is cone or pyramid-shaped. The famous Islamic tombs in India are the Taj Mahal at (Agra) Humayun Tomb (Delhi) Sher Shah Sur (Bihar) Jamia Masjid (Delhi) Hazratbal (Srinagar) and many others in different parts of the country. Moreover, the rulers various Islamic countries built many palaces, but only a few of these structures remain. Of the later ones, the best known is the Alhambra at Granader, Spain, built from 1248 to 1354.[54] There are still other famous palaces which include the palaces of the Mughal emperors of India in Agra, Delhi, Lucknow, Lahore, Hyderabad (Pakistan),all built in the 1600 A.D. Other examples of Islamic architecture include inns called *khans*; large fortified rest houses along trade routes; hospitals; and market streets or *bazaars* (in Arabic called *sooks*). In fact Islamic architecture has many unique features. Perhaps the most original is the *muqarnas-vault*, a stalactite-like honeycomb ceiling in which up to 5,000 small carvings are set at angles to each other.[55] In Muslim architecture, generally, construction with stone materials was much favoured, although rubble and brick was also used. It has been observed that it was brickwork which dominated all Muslim architecture, resulting in an aesthetic of applied decoration for ornamental effect, rather than a monumental plastic code. Muslim architecture has a radiant cultural history and owes its remarkable unity to a religious faith.

(d) Decorative Arts :

We shall deal decorative arts in some detail in the Third Chapter of the project. Here a brief survey is deemed in the fitness of things. Islamic art has a distinctive feature in the field of decoration. Islam is not simply a religion but a way of life. It deals with all aspects of human life and tries to satisfy man's natural urges and needs.

(i) Carpet Art (Rugs) :

In the field of decorate arts the carpet art has a significant importance in Islamic art world. Traditionally, people the followers of Islam sat or slept on rugs on the floor. islamic craft-workers developed carpet weaving into a fine art. Craft-workers used small lengths of various coloured threads of wool or silk to make knots into specific patterns. The knots created a pile with a richly decorated surface. Some of the finest silk rugs have 1,000 knots per square inch (approximately 60 per square centimeter). Sometimes craft-workers brocaded the rugs with gold and silver. The main areas of rug production in the Muslim world were central Asia, Turkey, Iran, and the Caucasus region of Russia. Iran is the most popular country in this field of art.

(ii) Textile Art :

In Islamic art the textile form has a great artistic significance. Basically the textiles art under the Abbasids, Tulunids and the Fatimids of Egypt (in 2nd to 6th Century A.D.), the Ayyubid and Mumluk dynasties; and the Iranian flourished and got much appreciation from the great aestheticians of the world. Muslim skillful technicians and weavers were used to engaged themselves in the development of this art. They taught and practiced the weaver's art into royal factories, which were technically known as *Tiraz* factories. These factories were established throughout the territorial possessions of the Caliphs to make this art popular and useful. In Iran during the earlier period Merv and Nishapur housed these famous '***Tiraz***' factories for the development to textile art in Islamic world.[56]

The art of weaving on a loom reached a high development in Islamic countries. Fine textile date from the 700's (A.D.) on. They were used for clothing, for such decorative elements as wall hangings and coverings, for gifts, and even for tents. Many were woven with silk thread. Early fabrics had designs based on those used in silks of pre-Islamic Persia. After the 1250's, craftworkers used chinese motifs. In the 1500's and 1600's, Persian weavers created scenes with figures inspired by contemporary miniature paintings. Other textiles used floral designs and geometric patterns. Persia is famous for her superb textile art.[57]

(iii) Metalware Art :

Muslim metal workers created superb objects of bronze or brass inlaid with copper, silver and gold. They were equally popular in this form of art like other forms such as carpet Textile, book-illunination, carving, glassware etc. Various designs have similarity among one another form of art. For example, "There are many links between designs on metal and the art of the book. In turn it would appear that pottery often imitated designs on metal".[58]

Few objects of gold or silver by Islamic artisans have been preserved. Islamic religious authorities have frowned on the use of precious metals. As a result, metal workers achieved beautiful effects by *chasing* (tracing) bronze or brass objects. They some-times inlaid one of these metals with copper, silver, or gold to form inscriptions or designs. At times, metal workers inlaid them with a black sulfuric alloy called niello. Artisans who worked with base metals usually chased or embossed them.[59] In metalwork the Sassanian tradition was the most popular in Iran. The early Islamic vessels consists mostly of trays and ewers fasnioned in the shape of animals and birds.[60]

(iv) The Art of Pottery :

In Islamic art forms the pottery has a distinctive creative feature of the Muslim artists. Consequently Islam brought important developments in manufacture and trade to the towns of the Middle East.[61] Pottery reached its highest development between the 800's (A.D.) and the 1300's (A.D.). Muslim artists developed many techniques that are still used today. For example, they engraved into slip, an earthy coating under the glaze, or else painted on the slip, and then added transparent glazes of many colours. These techniques were imiated by the Byzantine and Italian ceramists. Islamic potters also painted with a metallic pigment on a white or blue glaze to produce so-called *luster painting*. This difficult technique, practical in the Middle East and Spain from the 800 (A.D.) through the 1600 (A.D.) was also taken over by the potters of the Renaissance period in Italy.

There were the some main important centres of pottery-art in Egypt, Iraq, Syria, Turkey and Iran. Of all the centres of the ceramic-art, the Iran became the most famous, "Pottery furnishes perhaps the most comprehensive record of the artistic life of Islamic Persia"[62]. We shall discuss in detail the Islamic art of pottery in the Third Chapter of this project at present these introductory remarks seem sufficient.

(v) Glassware Art :

The Muslim artisans learnt various designs and techniques of decorating glass from the local artists. In this connection Syria and Egypt were the famous centres in execution of glass-ware. Further, the Iranian artists following in the foot steps of their Sassanion masters also continued and created different forms and decorative features in this field.

The glassware of the early Islamic period consists mainly of bottles, flasks, cups and receptacles for oils and perfume. Though the early work was not so decorative yet the creative artisans, with their aesthetic sensibility and the passage of time, learnt the art of decoration creating beauty in their products.[63]

Moreover, glassware art was used for mosque lamps, drinking utensils, vases, and windows. Artirans practiced most of the processes of glassmaking known since ancient times. The finest Islamic glassware has relief designs of animals and arabesques. Glass-making flourished in Iraq, Persia, and Egypt from 700's (A.D.) th 1100's (A.D.). Syrian glassmakers became famous in the 1200's (A.D.) and 1300's (A.D.) for the glass bottles, drinking vessels, and mosque lamps decorated with coloured enamels. Builders used richly coloured glass windows in many buildings, especially in mosques and private mansions.

(vi) The Art of Book-Illustration and Book-Binding :

(a) Book-Illustration :

In the Islamic art-world the book-illustration emerged as an important form of art and in this field Persian played a vital role. The Perisan artists had rich literary and cultural traditions due to which they very keenly illustrated some most important Persian books in which spiritual, ethical, social, cultural and aesthetical elements did figure. Mainly, the works of the four of the greatest Persian poets — Fird-ausī, Nizāmī. Ḥafiz and Sa'adī — became the subject-matter of the Persian artists for illustration. In these and other book-illustrations the Muslim artists also painted miniatures on plants, animals, human figures and other natural objects :

> Although there are examples of early wall paintings, better-known Islamic painting originated as book illustrations. Most of

> the earliest remaining examples date from after 1200. The Persians had rich literary traditions, and illustrated many poems, such as the epic *Shah-Namah* (*Book* of *Kings*), by the poet Firduasi. They also chose the *Qunitet* (*Khamsah*) by the poet Nizami and the poems and prose works by Sa'adi, including the Bostan (*Fruit Garden*) and *Gulistan* (*Rose Garden*). Another popular subject was a book of fables, *Kalila and Dimna*, which came from an Indian collection, the *Panchatantra*. Artists also painted miniatures in books on plants, animals, and constellations.[64]

Persia developed several styles and techniques in the field of book-illustration. The greatest period in Persian arts extended from 13th century to the late 16th century (A.D.). There were many artists in this field but the work of the best known Persian painter Kaml al-Dīn Bihazad deserves special mention here. He illustrated famous manuscripts with miniatures in the late 1400's (A.D.). During the late 1500's (A.D.) artists in India began to produce a more realistic style of painting. They gave much attention to paint those portraits which were kept in albums. The Tukish painters during the same period concentrated on illustrating historical works in the best realistic manner. (See Plate **9, 10, 13, 15**).

It is generally accepted that manuscripts of the Holy Qur'ān never had decorations showing human figures or animals. The Muslim artists or painters decorated the sacred Book —The Qur'ān with graceful scrolls and floral ornaments around the beautifully written texts.[65]

Manuscript-illumination was also one of the important forms of Islamic art. Muslim artists from Iraq, Egypt, Central Asia and Iran created various magnificent designs with beautiful colour schemes to illuminate the Holy

Qur'ān, in particular, and other religious or mystical and literary works in general :

> Originally the Qur'ān was not illuminated at all, but it was soon felt necessary to mark the beginning of a book, a chapter or a verse. This initially took the form of modest panels at the beginning of a book, palmette designs in the margin at the beginning of a chapter and small rosettes between verses. The designs are taken from a Qur'ān written in the year 1000 in Baghdad. The repertoire of motifs reflects the mixture of traditions and styles available to the artist at the centre of the Islamic worlds at that time: lotus designs from China and Egypt, scrolls of split palmettes, palmette flowers and rosettes form the Mediterranean classical tradition; and the winged, beaded and feathered designs of the Sasanian tradition from central Asia and Iran. These decorations subsequently became more lavish; frontispieces covered entire pages with intricate geometrical designs, the spaces filled with leaf scrolls, the interlaced borders decorated in gold, blue and red.[66]

(Please see some design with regard to the **illumination** of the Qur'ān i.e. Plates : **19, 20, 21, 23, 24, 26**).

(b) Book-binding :

Though the art of book-binding is not so popular as the art of book-illumination yet it has an important place in Islamic decorative arts. It is obvious that a book-binder had played a very important role in the preservation of valuable manuscripts before the press made it possible to produce copies of valuable works. So the Muslim scholars and *litterateurs* felt this need to ensure that valuable manuscripts are not destroyed or damaged by the passage of time and the art of book-bi^n^ding emerged as a seprate form.

The earliest book-covers of the Muslim period were made by the Egyptian artists most probably during the 2nd to the 5th century (A.D.)[67]. Again this art reached its zenith under the Timurids. In this connection the artists of the Herat Academy deserve special mention here who executed leather work of great beauty and distinction. For the most Muslim artists of this field leather was the ideal material for book-binding and colours made the art of Islamic book-binding matchless :

> Islamic books are enclosed in delicately worked leather bindings, which nearly always have a flap on the lower cover to be folded over all the pages. Persian craftworkers made bookbindings with molded or tooled designs on the outside and cut out patterns on the inside. Some of these date back to the 1400's (A.D.). Beginning in the mid-1200's (A.D.) many bookbindings had part of their designs imprinted in gold. Experts consider Islamic book-bindings to be among the most beautiful bindings ever produced.[68]

Muslim artists in book-binding tried to create decorative value in their art. We find this aspect quite vivid under the Safawid period. Persia again become the centre of this art of book-binding. Though Turkish artists followed the footsteps of their Persian co-workers yet their work, being beautiful, could not get that importance which the Iranian product had. Briefly, it can be said with confidence that the West is indebted to the East in the fields of book-binding and illumination and the Irarian craftworkers or artists deserve special appreciation in these forms of Islamic Art :

> It is necessary to point out that book-binding and illumination in the West is indebted to the East. The Italian painters, book-binders, and artists, especially in Venice in the late ninth/fifteenth

> and tenth/sixteenth centuries, imitated Eastern technique, especially that of the Irarian craftsmen, and through theme many Oriental motifs and decorative features were introduced in the West, the book-binding of which today is the envy of the East.[69]

Thus in the field of Islamic art some important forms such as calligraphy, architecture, miniature painting and decorative arts make this field distinctive and Muslim artists with their creative and aesthetically rich tradition contributed a lot in the world history of art. Islamic art in its true spirit, is divinely inspired and oriented art and therefore its approach is mystical one.

(C) THE RELATION BETWEEN ISLAMIC ART AND ISLAMIC WORLD-VIEW:

Islam is one of the greatest religious of the world. It's approach to human life as well as human spirituality is some what different from that of other religions such as Hinduism, Buddhism. Judaism and Christianity. There is no object or model of the Supreme Reality in Islamic art-world to be painted or portrayed as in case of other religions. However, the consequent Void has its distinctive significance in the Islamic art-world. *Al-Tawḥīd* (Unity of Being) is the essence of Islam and this metaphysical principle or Unity is the spiritual significance of the Void which is the only goal and soul of Islamic art. *Allah* is not seen like an object but He is realized as the Supreme Creator of everything. He has bestowed upon man the power of wisdom and creativity.

The independence and originality of Islamic art can directly be traced from its specific world-view. There is an indispensable relation between the

Islamic revelation and Islamic art. God is the source of all and He is the Knower of all things. Therefore, the essences or forms of all things have their reality in the Divine Intellect. Generally, the work of art, as we know, is an organised complex of sensuous and expressive elements, and its organisation is its form. But in Islamic art man's spiritual dimension has been overemphasized. All art and thought have been derived form this very emphasis. According to Seyyed Hossein Nasr, it is in reality the inner dimension of Islam, to the *batin* as contained in the Way and elucidated by the Truth, that one must turn for the origin of Islamic art. This inner dimension is moreover inextricably related to Islamic spirituality. Man's inwardness has been given much value in Islam. Moreover it is within the inner dimension of the Islamic tradition that one must seek the origins of Islamic art and the power which has created different 'forms' and sustained them over the ages.

The Qur'ān and the prophetic *Ḥadīth* (tradition) are the main sources of Islamic philosophy as well as Islamic art. All forms of art must be created in the light of the Qur'ān and the Traditions of the Prophet. The Qur'an emphasises the doctrine of Unity while the prophet provides the manifestation of this Unity into multiplicity and the witness to this unity in His creation. In this connection Seyyed Hossein Naṣr says :

> The twin sources of Islamic spirituality are the Qur'ān, in its inner reality and sacramental presence, and the very substance of the soul of the Prophet which has remained as an invisible presence within the Islamic world, not only through his Hadith within the hearts of those who have sought air which the invokers of His Blessed Name have breathed and still breathe. The origin

> of Islamic art must be sought in the inner realities (*ḥaqāiq*) of the Qur'ān which are also the principal realities of the cosmos and the spiritual reality of the Prophetic Substance from which flows the 'Muhammadan grace' (*al-barakat al-mubammadiyyah*). The Qur'ān provides the doctrine of Unity While the Prophet provides the manifestation of Unity in multiplicity and the witness to this Unity in His creation. For who would be able to testify to *La-ilaha illa'Llah* if there were no *Muhammad un rasul Allah*? Wherever the Muhammadan *barakah* has flowed and still flows, there one must seek the origin of the very creative act which has made the sacred art of Islam possible, for only by virtue of this *barakah* has it been possible to crystallize in the world of form, time, and space the *ḥaqāiq* which the Qur'ān contains within its inner dimension.[70]

Thus, the Holy Qur'ān and the prophetic grace (*barakah*) are the two primordial sources of Islamic art and thought. Without these two fountains there would be no Islamic art. Therefore, the relation between Islamic art and Islamic world-view or spirituality is essentially indispensable and unique. The art of Islam is Islamic art not because it was created by Muslims but because it issues forth from the Islamic revelation as do the Divine law and the way. This art crystallizes in the world of forms the inner realities of the Islamic revelation and issues from the inner dimension of Islam revealing to man the Ultimate *Sanctum-Sanctorum* of Divine Revelation. In brief Islamic art is a fruit of Islamic spirituality from the point of view of its genesis and as an aid. It is a complement and support for the spiritual life from the vantage point of realization or return to the Origin—the *summum bonum* of human life.

Islamic art driver its content or subject-matter from Islamic spirituality in a direct manner. This connection is the sole element of creativity in Muslim world :

> This link with the form of the Islamic revelation does not detract from the truth that the origin of this art lies in the inner content and spiritual dimension of Islam. Those who have created objects of Islamic art over the ages have done so either by being able to gain a vision of that archetypal world, thanks to the means made available by the Islamic revelation and specifically the Muḥammadan *barakah*, or have been instructed by those who have had such a vision. For the supra-individual character of Islamic art cannot have been brought into being by simply individualistic inspiration or creativity. Only the Universal can produce the Universal. If Islamic art leads to the inner chamber of the Islamic tradition, it is because this art is a message from that inner chamber sent to those qualified to harken to its liberating message and also to provide a climate of peace and equilibrium for society as a whole in conformity with the nature of Islam.to create an ambience in which God is remembered wherever one turns.[71]

The source of Islamic philosophy and Islamic Art is the One***Allah***. In this way, the Islamic Art is solely based upon a knowledge which is itself of a spiritual nature :

> (This) knowledge referred to by traditional masters of Islamic Art as *ḥikmah* or wisdom. Since in the Islamic tradition with its gnostic mode of spirituality, intellectuality and spirituality are inseparable, being facets of the same reality, the *ḥikmah* upon which Islamic art is based is none other than the sapiential aspect of Islamic spirituality itself.[72]

The relation between Islamic art and Islamic spirituality is unique in the sense that God is the source of everything. He is the Creator and Sustainer of everything. In Islamic philosophy and Islamic Art the common element which dominates the both and has its central importance, is Islamic spirituality. This Islamic world-view inspires almost all the Muslim philosophers and aestheticians.

Sufism is another spiritual movement which has its significant role and impact on Islamic art. In one way or the other, Sūfī tradition remained a constant source of inspiration of all Islamic arts during different periods of Muslim history. The influence of Sufism on different art-forms, particularly poetry, provided enough religious background to many Muslim miniaturists and musicians of different Muslim dynasties. These artists tried to understand and highlight the spiritual significance in their creative products :

> Although the Sufis were naturally related to the mosque in their defense, of the *Shariah*, many of them being among the 'Ulama', they were also profoundly connected to political authority, not in submitting to the power of the world and its luxury or in composing panegyrics for the powerful, but in providing spiritual guidance and example for those who wielded power. While certain sufi orders kept aloof from political authority others permitted their members of accept even the highest offices. In any case the Sufi influence was strong in the domain of the arts for which the court acted as patron. It is enough to study the religious background of many miniaturists and musicians of the Safavid, Ottoman and Mogul dynasties to become aware of this fact. The 'feminine' arts supported by the courts are interiorizing by their very nature and of a highly spiritual quality. They possess unmistakable spiritual traits which could not come about except through the presence of the influence of Islamic esoterism. Through an inner complementarily between the mosque and the court, both contributed to the creation of forms of Islamic art which are complementary in nature while sometimes combining in the creation of single works such as the royal mosques, some of which are among the greatest masterpieces of Islamic art.[73]

The upshot of the above discussion is that the link between Islamic art and Islamic spirituality is integral and essential. This relationship of Islamic art to the inner dimension of Islam or Islamic world-view has been demonstrated by different Muslim artists in almost all art forms such as **calligraphy, architecture, poetry, music, painting, decorative arts** etc. Islam claims to be a universal religion and it carefully deals with every sphere of human life. *Al-Tawḥīd* (Unity of Being) is the essence of Islam "Islam's claim to universality follows from the emphasis on the Unity of God. It holds that as a religion valid for all times, it must reveal the eternal nature of Truth. Truth cannot be changed though the processes of time may overlay it with accretion that hide or distort its real nature."[74] Islam emphasized Unity of the God-head in all art and though in a manner which has rarely been equaled by any other world's great religion.

Thus, Islam is noted for its emphasis on the unity of all aspects of life. It recognizes no distinction between politics and religion, economics and worship, ethics and aesthetics, thought and action, and between social and spiritual life.[75]

In brief, Islamic art is the result of the manifestation of Unity upon the plane of multiplicity. It reflects in its own distinctive manner the Unity of the Divine Principle—the dependence of all multiplicity upon the One**Allah**. This art makes manifest, in the physical Order directly perceivable by the senses, the archetypal realities and acts. Therefore, it is a ladder for the journey of the soul from the audio-visual world to the invisible supermundane or supernatural which is also silence transcending all sound.

REFERENCES

1. *The world Book Encyclopedia*, A Scolt Fetzer Co., London. Vol. 10, 1990, p. 463.
2. 'Alī, Syed Amīr, *The Spirit of Islam*, B.I. Publications, Delhi, 1978, pp. 137-8.
3. *The Holy Qur'ān*, (Text Translation and Commentary by A. Yusuf 'Alī), Published by Amana Corp. (Printed in U.S.A.), 1983, Surah 49:10.
4. *The Holy Qur'ān, op. cit.*, Surah 26:192 & 193.
5. *The Holy Qur'ān, op. cit.*, Surah 2:163-4.
6. *The Holy Qur'ān*, Surah 33:40.
7. *Ibid*, Surah 2:4 & 5.
8. *The World Book Encyclopedia, op. cit.*, p. 464.
9. A. Yusuf 'Alī (Commentary) *The Holy Qur'ān, op. cit.*, p. 18.
10. 'Umaruddin, M., *The Ethical Philosophy of Al-Ghazzālī*, Faculty of Art Publication Series-9, Aligarh Muslim University, Aligarh. 1962, p. 43.
11. *The Holy Qur'ān*, Surah 4:36.
12. *Ibid.*, Surah 25:67.
13. *Ibid.*, Surah 16:90.
14. *Ibid.*, Surah 3:134
15. *Ibid.*, Surah 49:13.
16. *Ibid.*, Surah 17:23.
17. *Ibid.*, Surah 7:199.

18. *Ibid.*, Surah 4:106.

19. *Ibid.*, Surah 5:9.

20. *Ibid.*, 107:123.

21. *Ibid.*, Surah 70:29 and Surah 79:40.

22. Umaruddin, M., *op. cit.*, p. 44.

23. *The Holy Qur'ān, op. cit.*, Surah 4:99.

24. *Ibid.*, Surah 7:199.

25. *The World Book Encyclopedia, op. cit.*, p. 465.

26. Iqbāl, S.M., *The Reconstruction of Religious Thought in Islam*, Shaikh Muhammad Ashraf, Kashmiri Bazar, Lahore, 1962, (preface) p. *V.*

27. Umaruddin, M., *op. cit.*, pp. 134-4.

28. *The Holy Qur'ān*, Surah 16:90

29. *Ibid.*, Surah 49:9.

30. *The Holy Qur'ān*, Surah 3:18.

31. *Ibid.*, Surah 4:135.

32. *Ibid.*, Surah 38:26.

33. *Ibid.*, Surah 67:2.

34. *Ibid.*, Surah 3:169.

35. *Ibid.*, Surah 2:154.

36. 'Alī, Syed Ameer, *op. cit.*, p. 138.

37. *Ibid.*, p. 138.

38. Richard. E. and Oleg G., *The Art and Architecture of Islam: 650-1250*, Penguin Books Ltd., England,1987, p.17.

39. *Ibid.*, p. 17.

40. *The Holy Qur'ān*, Surah 37:6

41. *Ibid.*, Surah 15:16.

42. Zainul 'Abedīan S., "Islam and the FIne Arts" in *Islamic Though* (Fine Arts Special), Editors M.N. Siddiqi and F.R. Faridi, Vols. 2 and 3, Nos. 1 and 6, May, 1956, p.6.

43. *Ibid.*, p. 6.

44. Nasr, Seyyed Ḥ., *Islamic Art and Spirituality*, Golgonooza Press, Sufflok, 1987, p. 17.

45. *The World Book Encyclopedia, op. cit.*, p. 467.

46. Nasr, Sayyed Ḥ., *op. cit.*, p. 4.

47. *The World Book Encyclopedia, op. cit.*, p. 467.

48. *Ibid.*, pp. 467-8.

49. Wilson, E., *Islamic Designs*, British Museum Publications, London, 1988, p. 14.

50. Bamborough P., *Treasures of Islam*, Arco Publishing Company. Inc., New York, p. 24.

51. *The World Book Encyclopedia, op. cit.*, p. 468.

52. Tomory, E., *A History of Fine Arts in India and the West*. Orient Longman Ltd. New Delhi, 1982, p. 142.

53. *Ibid.*, 468.

54. *Ibid.*, p. 469.

55. *Ibid.*, p. 469.

56. Sharif, M.M., (ed.) *A History of Muslim Philosophy,* (Vol. II) Otto Harrassowitz Wiesbaden, Germany, (Pub. Pakistan Philosophical Congress, 1966), pp. 1186-7.

57. *The World Book Encyclopedia, op. cit.*, p. 470.

58. Wilson, E., *Islamic Designs, op. cit.*, p. 14.

59. *The World Book Encyclopedia, op. cit.*, p. 470.

60. Sharif, M.M., *op. cit.*, p. 1190-92.

61. Wilson, E., *Islamic Designs, op. cit.*, p. 12.

62. Pope, A.U., *op. cit.*, p. 1446.

63. Sharif, M.M., *op. cit.*, p. 1183.

64. *The World Book Encyclopedia, op. cit.*, p. 470.

65. *Ibid.*, p. 470.

66. Wilson. E., *Islamic Designs, op. cit.*, p. 12.

67. Sharif, M. M., *op. cit.*, p. 1183.

68. *The World Book Encyclopedia, op. cit.*, p. 470.

69. Sharif, M. M., *op. cit.*, p. 1183.

70. Nasr, S.H., *op. cit.*, p. 6.

71. *Ibid.*, pp. 7-8.

72. *Ibid.*, p. 8.

73. *Ibid.*, pp. 12-3.

74. Kabir, Humayun, *Science, Democracy and Islam.* George Allen and Unwin Ltd., London, 1955, p. 16.

75. Nasr. S. H., *op. cit.*, p. 15-6.

CHAPTER II

IRANIAN PAINTING

(A) **Sacred Art in Persian Culture**

(B) **Iranian Influence on Islamic Art**

CHAPTER - II

IRANIAN PAINTING

(A) SACRED ART IN PERSIAN CULTURE :

By **'sacred'** we mean 'pious' or dedicated to religious use or 'hallowed'. It is pertaining or related to deity, religion or hallowed places, buildings, books, personalities, things etc. In Islamic art the word 'sacred' is used to represent every art form in relation to 'spirituality'.

In the history of Islam, one of the major contributors to Islamic philosophy and civilization and especially to art has been Persia. It played an important role in the development of Islamic art forms. It is the greatness of Persia where the principles of the sacred art of Islam in relation to spirituality can be demonstrated amply in many fields and domains of art, both plastic and sonoral. Persian art, at once deeply Persian and Islamic, represents a culmination of Islamic art and one of its indispensable peaks.[1]

Persians are famous for their aesthetic sensibility. They have been deeply spiritually motivated people and in the creation of their numerous remarkable works of Islamic art, we clearly see the elements of Islamic revelation. The sacred art of Islam has been a dominant factor in the Persian culture. In this regard Seyyed Hossein Nasr writes :

> The highly artistic nature of Persians and their love for beauty, refinement, and delicacy enabled them not only to create one of the great schools of art in the ancient world associated with the Achaemenians. Parthians and Sassanids, but also to absorb and

> apply the principles of the Islamic revelation in the creation of numerous outstanding works of Islamic art. Both because of its richness, variety, and depth of expression. Persian Islamic art presents an ideal field for the study of the sacred art of Islam in relation to Islamic spirituality on the one hand and to the ethos and genius of a particular people and culture on the other.[2]

Persian art has an important historical aspect. This art shows the most fundamental and characteristic activity of the people of Iran. Their valuable contribution to world civilization in general and Islamic art in particular deserve appreciation. The essential record of their lives and the history of their art which highlights many problems in the history of human culture, require special attention. According to Arthur Upham Pope :

> Art was an essential element in that first of all civilization, which emerged on the Iranian plateau more than six thousand years ago, and it played a vital role in all subsequent ages, maintaining throughout a well defined individuality. Early achieving high quality, it has produced a long series of masterpieces in many media and in a succession of varied but organically related styles.[3]

It is rightly said that in Asia, Iran had been a potent force scores of centuries earlier. Its early emergence, long career, and persistent high quality, all make Persian art significant as a phase of general cultural history. Because highly evolved arts appear on the Iranian plateau with the first developed civilization, they may help to determine how primitive and how fundamental is the aesthetic impulse, and in gauging its character, function. and survival value. The study of such a persistent artistic production should reveal the principal motives that support it, and throw light on the nature of artistic individuality. Because it is evident that religion presided at the birth of art in this region, and in some form sustained it through its maturity, it offers testimony bearing on the significant and not wholly elucidated relation between these two fundamental and eternal concerns of humanity.

The art of Iran is a record and an interpretation of a people that since earliest times played an influential and inspiring role in the history of the world. Through this art we can easily understand the socio-cultural, religio-political as well as the aesthetical aspects of those people.[3]

In Iran the principles of sacred art of Islam in relation to spirituality have been demonstrated in different forms of art. In following pages we shall briefly discuss the sacred art in Persian Culture.

So far as the sacred or hallowed art is concerned we must understand the traditional view of reality in both physical and metaphysical worlds. According to the traditional view of the Universe, reality has many phases. It embodies or incorporates various levels or stages. The One 'God' or '***Allah***' is the source of them all. Reality possesses several levels of existence mainly the (1) angelic world, (2) the psychic world and (3) the physical world. Though man lives in the material world, yet at the same time he is surrounded by all of the higher levels of existence above it. Traditional man lives in the awareness of this reality. Though he is hardly aware of metaphysical and cosmological questions. The sacred art is considered as the bridge between the spiritual and material world. This art essentially comes from the spiritual world and harks back to that world. It is simultaneously a two-way traffic from and to the realm of spirit, so to say :

> The sacred marks an eruption of the higher worlds within the psychic and material planes of existence, of eternity in the temporal order, of the Centre in the periphery. All that comes directly from the spiritual world—which stands above the psychic world and must never be confused with it, the one being *ruh* (spirit), and the other *nafs* (soul) in Islamic parlance – is sacred, as is all that serves as a vehicle for the return of man to the spiritual world. But this possibility namely return to the realms beyond, is inseparable from the reality of the descent from above, because essentially only that which comes from the spiritual world can act as the vehicle to return to the world. The sacred, then, marks the 'miraculous' presence of the spiritual in the material, of Heaven on earth. It is an echo from Heaven to remind earthly man of his heavenly origin.[4]

The sacred art has very important place in Persian Culture. To understand more clearly the role of sacred art in Persian Culture we must know the traditional Persian art. It must be remembered that in the case of Persia Traditional' and 'Sacred' are inseparable. But at the same time we must note that they are not identical as Hossein Nasr remarks :

> The quality termed 'traditional' pertains to all the manifestations of a traditional civilization reflecting the spiritual principles of that civilization both directly and indirectly. 'Sacred', however, especially as used in the case of art, must be reserved for those traditional manifestations which are directly connected with the spiritual principles in question, hence with religious and initiatic rites and acts possessing a sacred subject and a symbolism of a spiritual character. Opposed to the sacred stands the profane and opposed to the traditional, the anti-traditional.[5]

The art is inestimably valued in Persian culture. In Persia, Qur'ānic Calligraphy is sacred art while the miniature is traditional art reflecting the principles of Islam in a more indirect manner. In Persian Culture the very words such as *fann*, 'فن' *hunar*, 'هنر' *san'at* 'صنعت' etc.. used for art reveal its universality by pointing out different aspects of life. Even now-a-days these words are used to denote the capability of 'doing' or 'creating' or 'making' something correctly.

All such verses of the Holy Qur'ān which encourage human creative ability and aesthetic sensibility have been highlighted through different art-techniques. The basic contention regarding the sacred art in Persian culture is that one cant's create sacred art without penetrating himself deeply into that religion or to the *sanctum sanctorum* of spiritual world. Therefore, throughout the Persian history, an intimated relation has existed between art and spiritual discipline deriving from the religion then and now dominant in Persia. In fact, the examples, symbols etc. of Pre-Islamic Persia in which we see how religion was the dominant factor. Religions such as Zoroashtrianism, Mathraism and Manichalism left their impact on Iranian life but we cannot say with confidence about their relationship with sacred art.

The connection between art and spiritual principles is more firmly established and clear during the Islamic period. In almost all the art-forms we find the spiritual element as a dominant force. The Qur'anic calligraphy, Sufi-poetry, music, architecture, the Sword (*Dhu'lfiqār* or *Zulfiqār*) of 'Alī, *Ta'ziyah*, Horse of *Kerbla* (*Dhuljanāḥ* or *Zuljanāḥ*), etc. are sacred in Persian Culture. Persians consider their language too, as sacred, because it was born during the early Islamic period and therefore, had a greater degree of freedom to convey the message of the Holy Book (The Qur'ān) in its true spirit. The

Persian poetry reflects a 'Spiritual style' the message of which is related to the Islamic revelation :

> In the realm of the audible the sacred art *par excellence* in Islam is of course the chanting and recitation of the Qur'ān, which is the spiritual force behind the poetry and music of all Islamic peoples. The Persian language as we know it today was born during the early Islamic period and hence had a greater degree of freedom to be molded by the spirit and form of the Qur'ān that even Arabic, which at least in the realm of poetry was already formed at the time of the Qur'ānic revelation. This fact, added to the poetic genius of the Persians, is the reason for the remarkable richness of religious and mystical poetry in Persian. Persian poetry is not sacred art in a direct sense, but it is an inspired traditional art of an elevated order connected intimately with the Qur'ān. This is true especially of Persian Sufi poetry. It can be said, in fact, that if Arabic is the language of the 'Word'—the language of God as He spoke through Gabriel to the Prophet of Islam—Persian is the language of the angels. It is the language of paradise, and the beauty of Persian poetry is a reminiscence of paradisal joy. The rhyme and rhythm poetry reflects a 'spiritual style' that of Persian relates it to the form of the Qur'ān as the massage of this poetry is related to the content of the Qur'ānic revelation.[6]

Persian poetry has a very significant role in Persian Culture. It has spiritual message to convey. Persian Poetry in its rhyme and rhythm, as mentioned earlier, reflects the echo of the Holy Book (The Qur'ān) in the minds of men and women who created this art. The poets like Rūmī, Ḥāfiz, Sa'adī, 'Aṭṭār, Jāmī, etc. mainly composed Sūfī poetry. According to these poets poetry is the result of the imposition Spiritual and Intellectual principles upon the matter or substance of language. In reality poetry bears an Intellectual and Spiritual message. Highlighting poetry in this context, Seyyed Ḥossein Naṣr refers to the Persian Sūfī Poet 'Abdal-Raḥmān Jāmī who defines poetry in the following words :

شعر چبود؟ نوای مرغ خرد　　شعر چبود؟ مثال ملك ابد
می شود قدر مرغ از او روشن　　که به گلخن درست یا گلشن
می سراید زگلشن ملکوت　　می کشد زان حریم قوت و قوت

> What is poetry? the song of the bird of the Intellect.
> What is poetry? The similitude of the world of eternity.
> The value of the bird becomes evident through it,
> And one discovers whether it comes from the oven of a bath house or a rose garden.
> It composes poetry form the Divine rose garden;
> It draws its power and sustenance from that sacred precinct.[7]

Thus, the classical Persian poetry is also considered as 'sacred art' in Persian culture. It has in it the highest spiritual value which, on the contrary, 'new poetry' lacks :

> Be that as it may, it is essential to remember that classical Persian poetry, especially in its Sufi form, is a traditional art of the highest value and of a spiritual and even therapeutic nature, and that its destruction by the 'new poetry' is no less than the destruction of a poetry of celestial quality by a poetry that is purely terrestrial and often unintelligible. Some of the talented younger poets have written 'new poetry' which has some earthly beauty, but the pales into insignificance before the suprapersonal, heavenly beauty which the very forms of classical poetry, not to speak of its symbolism and content, make possible.[8]

The music is another important form of sacred art in Persian culture. The spiritual states evoked by the classical Persian music are closely related to the spiritual states (*aḥwāl* 'احوال') of the Sufis, and through Sūfī-tradition to the spirit of the Holy Scripture (The Qur'ān) :

> As for music, the music of Persia, although influenced by different musical traditions especially the ancient Egyptian, has its origins

> in the music of the ancient Aryan peoples and is akin to the Greek music heard by Pythagoras. But during the Islamic period it grew in a distinct manner and in a more contemplative direction, not in spite of but because of Islam as we shall have occasion to discuss more fully later. By banning the social aspect of music, especially in cities where the inciting of passions caused by music can always lead to greater moral degradation than in the countryside. Islam turned classical music in an inward direction, as a contemplative art. The spiritual states evoked by classical Persian music are closely related to the spiritual states (ahwal) of the Sufis, and through Sufism to the spirit of the Qur'ān. In both its purely musical content, as well as in the Suifi poetry with which it has always been intimately connected. Persian music represents a spiritual art of a high order, a powerful aid in the attainment of the contemplative states of Sufism. It is not accidental that the Sufis have cultivated the mystical sessions of music and even dance (*samā*), and that one (Maulānā Jalāl al-Dīn Rūmī) of the greatest Sufi masters and revelers of the esoteric meaning of the Qur'ān.[9]

Seyyed Ḥossein Naṣr further refers to Maulānā Jalāl al-Dīn Rūmī, who founded a Sūfī-Order well known for its music and dancing (the *Mawlawis*) could openly say :

> The musician began to play before the drunken Turk,
> Behind the veil of melody the mysteries of the eternal
> connivent between God and Man.[10]

Maulānā Rūmī points out that music has a divine influence. It is a source of ecstasy. 'Ecstasy' or its another equivalent Arabic word *fanā'* (Self abnegation) finds prominent mention in the Sufi-tradition. It is the way to union with God. The *samā'*, which is a primordial source of it (*fanā'* or *Wiṣāl*), "literally means 'audition' ". But here in Rūmī's Sufism it includes music's singing and dancing[11]. It plays a very significant role in the context of ecstasy.

according to Maulànà Rũmī. In Persian culture the poetry has an important place and especially the poetry of Rumi has been regarded as sacred or spiritual one.

According to Rumi' music induced mental collectedness and intensifies the flame of love. It is, in reality, the food of lovers. K. Khosla beautifully explains the view point of Maulānā Rũmī about *Sama*ʿ in the following words:

> Explaining the inner significance of *Samā*ʿ in the *Dīwān* Rũmī says that *Samā*ʿ is to hear the sound of *balā* ('yes') affirming the Lordship of God at the Primal Covenant; it is to sever oneself from oneself; it is to attain to union with Him. It is to be unconscious of individual existence and savour everlasting life (baqā) in absolute self-extinction (fana-i-muṭlaq). It is to make the head like the ball before the stroke of His love, and run without head and foot.
>
> Speaking of Ibrahim, bin Adham, Rumi says that Ibrahim would listen to the sound of the rebeck, as it was to him an echo of the voice of God and he desired to recall His voice, proclaiming His lordship at the Primal Covenant. That voice is heard in the heart of the Sufi as trumpeting the spiritual resurrection, and it is like the blast of the Universal Trumpet that will be heard at the Resurrection.[12]

Most of the performers of Persian, Ṭurkish and Indian music have been associated with Sufism. It is, infact, the richness and depth of the Persian music which is appreciated by every one. "Only those with a contemplative dimension can benefit from the liberating power of this music which cuts man from the fetter of material existence and enables the bird of the human soul to fly with joy and freedom in the infinite horizons of the 'sky' of the spiritual world".[13]

Besides poetry, music and other sacred forms of art, a traditional type of art that is especially associated with Shi'ism and found in Persia as well as in other countries such as Iraq, Indo-Pakistani subcontinent, is *ta'ziyah*. It is usually different portraying extremely sad events of the tragedy of *Karbalā*. In fact, this religious theatre is the 'sacred' and closest art form in Islam. It has a tremendous historical background and possesses a religio-ethical and humanistic depth as well as the highest example of commitment of the Spiritual Entity :

> Nevertheless the *ta'ziyah* did develop as a religious art of power and beauty which has fulfilled certain religious needs of Shi'ism without its being essential to the ritual practices of Islam. An important character of the *ta'ziyah* that must always be remembered is that it can have efficacy and meaning only in the traditional context for which it was meant. The audience is as much a part of the play as the actors, and both participate with all their body and soul in the events of sacred history that are retold on the stage.[14]

Briefly, it can be said that Persian traditional art in general and sacred art in particular have left a heritage of unbelievable richness and inspiring depth for the Persian people. Islamic tradition has its own unique importance in all its dimensions, especially in its spiritual and artistic aspects. The vastly rich traditional heritage and sacred art of Persia, and infact, Islamic art as a whole, can rightfully help modern man to know the meaning and purpose of life in its true sense and to find out importance of relationships of God, man and the Universe :

> With awareness of traditional and sacred art, the work of the true artist, as well as scholar, can become like the song of the bird,

> heard above the sound and clamor that fatigues and sickens the soul of man. It can become the means to remind man of the peace, tranquillity, and joy for which he was created and which he seeks at all times knowingly or unknowingly but which he can only find when he gains an awareness of the sacred and accepts that he must surrender himself to the Will of Heaven.[15]

All the Persian mystical poets have equal importance and respect in Persian culture. Their poetry is considered as sacred because it imbibes spiritual element in its essence. Most famous Persian poets such as Sana'i (whose best known work is the *Ḥadiqatul Ḥaqīqat* (Garden of Truth); Shaikh Faridud-Dīn 'Aṭṭār (best know for his *Mantiqut-Ṭair* (Conference of the Birds); Jalāl al-Dīn Rūmī (most famous for his *Mathnawī*); Sa'adī (popularly known for his two works *Gulistān* and *Bostān*); Ḥafiz (popular for his *Dīwān*) and Firdaúsī for his *Shah-Nāmah*, have mystical approach in their writings. Iranian people use their collections to help plan their lives.[16]

This is a brief survey of the sacred Art in Persian culture. Now we shall take up Iranian influence on Islamic art and highlight some more important aspects of Persian art-tradition.

(B) IRANIAN INFLUENCE ON ISLAMIC ART :

Truth, beauty and goodness are the most important values in human life. To have them and love them is the natural urge of man. All artistic activity is a search for beauty. The love of beauty too lies embedded deep in human nature. It manifests itself in diverse forms and at various levels, but it finds its profoundest expression in the creation of art. No system of thought and no code of conduct which claims to be based on a knowledge of human nature could afford either to ignore or immolate this basic human urge, viz; aesthetic sensibility.

Islam, being the natural religion, not only gives this natural urge (creation and appreciation of art and beauty) a recognition, but categorically seeks to evoke and encourage it in many ways. Thus, Islamic art is the art of the civilization based on Islamic principles. Islamic art, no doubt, is the result of various ingredients and influences especially from the pre-Islamic traditions. It is a fact that the Arabs themselves had little art though the elements of aesthetics are inherent in Islam itself. But through their constant conquests they come into contact with the highly developed arts of Persia or Iran, Syria, Egypt, Mesopotamia or Iraq and other civilizations. Thus people who accepted Islam blended these cultural influences and enthusiastically developed a distinct and fairly uniform style of art well-known as *Islamic Art*. Under the influence of Islam, the artists were stimulated to unfold their inner potentialities and capabilities, and excel themselves in all Islamic art forms :

> Islamic art is made up from many ingredients and influences especially from the pre-Islamic traditions which existed before the Arab conquest. From the Arab art of the desert to the vibrant art of the Steppes of Central Asia; from the native Persian and Egyptian traditions to those of Byzantium and the vegetative native art of India— all contributed to the overall richness of the art of Islam. There is an identity to Islamic art which can be seen throughout the Islamic countries. An element of order and of the infinite pattern. of the abstract and the figurative. Islamic art is all powerful and all embracing. It is not a religious art and yet at the same time it is. Under Islam, artists were stimulated to excel themselves in all the arts, employing their mastery over the discipline of writing. beautifying the word of God: in buildings

> both religious and secular, in pottery, metalwork, glass and textiles, and in the figurative miniature paintings, which, although not encouraged by Islam, were no doubt a direct result to Islamic culture. All these are, in addition to the religion itself — the real treasures of Islam.[17]

Of all the cultural influences on Islamic art, the most prominent and inspiring is Iranian one. In every walk of life Iran has her rich cultural and historical background. Iran is an ancient country in the Middle East region of southwestern Asia. It is a land of snow-capped mountains, green valleys and barren deserts. Iran is one of the world's oldest countries. Its history dates back almost 5000 years. In Biblical times, Persian Kings ruled a vast territory that inculded most of south western Asia and parts of Europe and Africa.[18]

From the above brief introduction about Iran it can easily be inferred that Persia has had rich cultural and artistic traditions. If some one studies the Iranian way of life one can fairly reach to this conclusion that aesthetic sensibility has been an essential part of their life. Iranian people have immense creative artistic abilities in almost all forms of art. This is the reason that their influence on Islamic art-forms deserves appreciation and special mention in the history of Islamic aesthetics.

We have already discussed Iranian art-tradition in the preceding part of this chapter, here this brief survey seems sufficient to pin-point that Iranian influence on Islamic art is undoubtedly great and predominent. It is a fact that throughout the long centuries of Islamic history one of the major inspiring forces of Islamic civilization and especially art has been Persia. The traditional **miniature painting**, **architecture**, **ceramics**. designs in **decorating buildings**.

roofs, walls etc. and all different Persian motifs, in the field of art, left an everlasting effect on Islamic art. Because a tradition embraces all of man's life and activities, so after embracing Islam, Iranian people made a radical attempt to Islamize all forms of art. Henceforth, the sacred and the traditional both art forms went together. In a sense, it is indispensable :

> It must first of all be remembered that 'traditional' and 'sacred' are inseparable, but not identical. The quality termed 'traditional' pertains to all the manifestations of a traditional civilization reflecting the spiritual principles of that civilization both directly and indirectly. 'Sacred,' however, especially as used in the case of art, must be reserved for those traditional manifestations which are directly connected with the spiritual principles in question, hence with religious and initiatic rites and acts possessing a sacred subject and a symbolism of a spiritual character.[19]

It is the greatness of Persian people who imbibed the Islamic principles with their traditional art-activity and contributed a lot under the title **'Islamic Art'** :

> ... Persia, where the principles of the sacred art of Islam in relation to spirituality can be demonstrated amply in many fields and domains of art, both plastic and sonoral. Perisn art, at once deeply Persian and Islamic, represents a culmination of Islamic art and one of its indisputable peaks. The highly artistic nature of Persians and their love for beauty, refinement, and delicacy enabled them not only to create one of the great schools of art in the ancient world associated with the Achaemenians, Parthians and Sassanids, but also to absorb and apply the principles of the Islamic revelation in the creation of numerous outstanding works of Islamic art. Both because of its richness, variety, and depth of expression.[20]

The highest creative and artistic nature of Persians and their aesthetic sensibility clearly show that throughout Persian history a close relationship has undoubtedly existed between art and spiritual discipline deriving from the religion then dominant in Persia. Though little is know about social life in pre- Islamic Persia, yet there are enough proofs to ascertain that such a link has clearly existed. Besides this link, we find more prominently the architectural forms, decorative arts and the gardens — all have a definite traditional character:

> Throughout Persian history an intimate relation has existed between art and the spiritual discipline deriving from the religion then dominant in Persia. Since little is known of the details of social organization in pre-Islamic Persia, the exact institutional link between the artisans and craftsmen and the priestly class is difficult to delineate. But the results are there to prove that such a link clearly existed. Nearly all important remnants of the art of that period are either religious or royal in character. And since the royalty was of a definite religious character, the royal art was in turn intimately connected with the Zoroastrian world-view. Even Persepolis, as has been suggested by A.U. Pope, seems to have been constructed as a palace for religious ceremonies rather than for the purely political activity of ruling over the empire. Moreover. the architectural forms and the gardens have a definite traditional and symbolic character, the garden being a form of mandala which closes upon an inner centre and serves as a 'reminder' and copy of 'paradise.' ... Suffice it to say. however, that in the case of Mani, painting was considered as the particular 'miraculous' gift of the founder of the religious movement himself.[21]

Briefly. it can rightly be said that Iran has a radiant cultural heritage and inspiring artistic tradition. There is an amazing influence on Islamic art. It is so because of the fact that Iran has long been famous for its architecture.

painting, and poetry. Early architects in Iran built magnificient mosques and palaces. They decorated the walls and domes with brightly coloured mosaic and tile designs. Traditional Persian painting features delicate detail work and jewel-like colours.

In every form of Islamic art Iranian impact obviously is a dominent factor. Iranian aesthetic sensibility and creative urge have made specific contribution to the enrichment of various art forms. Iranian craft-workers make beautiful jewelry, pottery, and metalware. Their handwoven Persian carpet arts or rugs are prized, praised and appreciated throughout the world for their graceful patterns and soft colours. The complicated designs of the rugs often require months of labour to complete. Other traditional arts in Iran include **embroidery, silk weaving. wood-carving. book-illustration, book-illumination** and **calligraphy**.[22]

REFERENCES

1. Nasr, Seyyed Ḥossein, *Islamic Art and Spirituality, Op. cit.*, p. 64.
2. *Ibid.*, p. 64.
3. Arthur Upham Pope & P. Ackerman, (editors), *A Survey of Persian Art*, vol. I Manafzadeh Group, Teheran, London. p. 1
4. Nasr, S. Ḥossein, *op. cit.*, p. 65.
5. *Ibid.*, pp. 65-6.
6. *Ibid.*, p. 76.

7. *Ibid.*, p. 91.

8. *Ibid.*, pp. 77-8.

9. *Ibid.*, p. 78.

10. cf. *Islamic Art and Spirituality* by Seyyed Ḥossein Nasr, *Op. cit.*, p. 78.

11. Khosla, K. *The Sufism of Rūmī*, Element Books, Great Britain, 1987, p. 193.

12. *Ibid.*, p. 195.

13. Nasr, S. Hossein, *op. cit.*, p. 79.

14. *Ibid.*, p. 79.

15. *Ibid.*, p. 82.

16. Khosla, K., *The Sufism of Rūmī, Op. cit.*, pp. 9-10, and *The World Book Encyclopedia, op. cit.*, p. 405.

17. Bamborough P., *Treasures of Islam, op. cit.*, pp. 19-20.

18. *The World Book Encyclopedia, op. cit.*, vol. 10, p. 400.

19. Nasr, S. Hossein, *op. cit.*, pp. 65-6.

20. *Ibid.*, p. 64.

21. *Ibid.*, pp. 69-70.

22. *The World Book Encyclopedia, op. cit.*, vol. 10, p. 405.

CHAPTER III

ISLAMIC ART IN IRAN

(A) Islamic Calligraphy
(B) Miniature Painting
(C) Decorative Arts

CHAPTER III

ISLAMIC ART IN IRAN

(A) ISLAMIC CALLIGRAPHY :

اِقْرَأْ بِاسْمِ رَبِّكَ الَّذِىْ خَلَقَ . اِقْرَأْ وَرَبُّكَ الْاَكْرَمُ . اَلَّذِىْ عَلَّمَ بِالْقَلَمْ . عَلَّمَ الاِنْسَانَ مَالَمْ يَعْلَمْ .

Read in the name of thy Lord and

Cherisher, Who created---

He Who taught the use of *Pen*,

Taught man that which he knew not.[1]

The above verses of the Qur'ān emphasize the importance of *'ilm* (knowledge) and *qalam* (pen). In the very first verses of the Chapter *al- 'Alaq* (the Clot) the Prophet Muhammad is ordered to 'read' 'اقرء' and make use of 'pen' 'قلم' . There is a special Chapter (*Surah*) entitled 'The Pen' (*al-qalam*) which opens with an Arabic letter *nun* 'ن' followed by the verses:

نٓ. وَالْقَلَمِ وَمَا يَسْطُرُوْنَ

'By the pen and that which they write'.[2]

Muslim scholars commonly agreed that the letter *nun* 'ن' in Arabic resembles an 'inkpot' which contains the ink with which the archetypes of all being are written upon the Guarded Tablet (*al-lawh al-Mahfūz* اللوح المحفوظ).[3]

Islamic calligraphy has a metaphysical foundation due to which it is considered as "Sacred art" in Islamic culture. Highlighting the spiritual basis of this art, Seyyed Ḥossein Nasr refers to the ninth/fifteenth century famous Persian Sufi scholar Kamal al-Din Husayn Kashifi who beautifully explains, in his Qur'anic commentary *Mawahib-i 'Aliyyah*, the mystical background of the above first verse of the Sura *al - qalam* saying that the initial letter '*nun*' is for 'light' (*al-nur*) which was the first reality created by *Allah* (according to the tradition) and the last letter '*al-Raḥmān*' stands for the Divine Mercy (by virtue of which all creation was brought forth). In this connection, he further refers to the views of the Persian Sūfī with regard to the spiritual significance of Islamic Calligraphy :

> Kashifi adds that God first created the *Qalam*, then the Inkpot or *nun* so that He begins the chapter of 'The Pen' with the lines '*nun* and the Pen'. According to another *ḥadith* the *Qalam* symbolizes the tongue and *nun* the mouth. The Supreme Pen, according to Kashifi is light whose 'extension is the distance between heaven and earth'. Kashifi also states that the letter *nun* is an allusion to the synthetic Divine knowledge contained in the All-Comprehensive Essential Unity (*ahadiyyat-i dhatiyya-yi jam 'iyyah*) and the Pen refers to the detailed Divine knowledge contained in the Celestial Unicity (*wahidiyyat-i Sama' iyyah*). 'What the Pen has written from the [ink] of the eternal ink-pot are the exalted, simple, Divine Letters as well as the inferior, compound, lordly words'. Kashifi thus summarizes the metaphysical foundation of calligraphy based upon the Qur'anic symbol of the Pen and Inkpot, of *nun* and *Qalam*, providing a key for the understanding of the metaphysical principle and spiritual significance of Islamic calligraphy and the role that calligraphy plays in the religious and artistic life of traditional Islam.[4]

The Holy Qur'ān is the source of every art - form according to the Muslim artists. They believe that the origin of the sacred calligraphy is the visual embodiment of the Sacred Word. The Divine Pen (*al-qalam*) wrote the realities of all things upon the Guarded Tablet, as mentioned earlier. The Noble Qur'ān itself further attests the writing material —'ink' —in the verse which says :

وَلَوْأَنَّمَا فِىْ ٱلْاَرْضِ مِنْ شَجَرَةٍ أَقْلَمٌ وَٱلْبَحْرُ يَمُدُّهُ مِنْ بَعْدِهِ سَبْعَةُ أَبْحُرٍمَّا نَفِدَتْ
كَلِمٰتُ اللّٰهِ إِنَّ اللّٰهَ عَزِيْزٌ حَكِيْمٌ

And if all the trees
On earth were pens
and the Ocean (were ink),
With seven Occans behind it
To add to its (supply),
Yet would not the Words
Of God be exhausted
(In the writing): for God
Is Exalted in power,
Full of Wisdom.[5]

This verse indicates, on the one hand, that the 'pen' and 'ink' are the source to acknowledge [God] *Allah* for His countless gifts bestowed upon human being; and on the other, His Words: the wonderful signs and Commandments are infinite and cannot be expressed if all the trees were made into pens, and all the wide Oceans, multiplied seven times. were made into ink.[6] Thus, the art of calligraphy, which reflects on the earthly plane the writing of God's Word upon the Guarded Tablet, is considered as the origin of the plastic arts. The Qur'ānic calligraphy owes its genesis to the Islamic revelation and, in reality, it is the response of the soul of the Muslims to the Divine Message :

> Qur'ānic calligraphy issues at once from the Islamic revelation and represents the response of the soul of the Islamic peoples to

> the Divine Message. The points traced by the Divine Pen created at once the celestial archetype of Qur'anic calligraphy as well as the lines and volumes of which the cosmic order is constituted and from which issues not only natural space, but also the space of Islamic architecture. In the mystery of the Point, represented by the diacritical point under the first letter which opens the Noble Qur'ān, namely the letter *ba*, is to be found the principle of both Islamic calligraphy and Islamic architecture, the principle of both the sonoral and plastic arts, the root of both of which is to be found in the Sacred Book. The points and lines of Islamic calligraphy with their inexhaustible diversity of forms and rhythms are related to that Supreme Divine Precinct at whose centre resides the first Point which is none other than His Exalted Word.[7]

Iran, being one of the ancient centres of art and culture, has had a rich heritage and has made enormous contribution to the enrichment of various Islamic art - forms. Although Iran is best known for its contribution to poetry, yet the contribution to graphic arts and calligraphy deserves special mention and appreciation. Besides other art-forms, the supermacy of Iran in the art of calligraphy has never been challenged. The 'Arabic calligraphy did vigorously developed in Persia owing to the spiritual temperament of Iranian Muslims. Almost all the artistic and religious ideals have been embaded in the beautiful writing :

> For more than twenty centuries writing has been a major medium for the expression of the Iranian genius, and of all the art it has been most sympathetic to Iran's aesthetic point of view, conveying more immediately her conception of spiritual beauty by means of pure form. Nearly all her artistic and religious ideals have been embodied in fine writing, not only in the great movements such as Manichaeism, but even in lesser sects, like the Babis, the tendency antedating the Arab conquest and prevailing throughout Islamic history even down to the present day, in a continuity that has never been seriously broken.[8]

The art of Calligraphy reflects the inner glory and strength of Islamic Revelation. The Persian artists find themselves spiritually involved in this fine art-form. Owing to their significance in Persian cultural tradition, the study of calligraphic styles becomes an aid to the historical research, but in order to yield its full significance (besides the spiritual) such a study must be undertaken from the two different angles — ***decorative*** and ***social***:

> On the one hand, the alphabets and the inscriptions composed from them can be understood and appreciated as decorative constructions. Calligraphy in this respect, constitutes one special phase of ornament, and because of its precise history and its exact and sensitive reflection of changes in taste and style it may serve as a useful guide in dating and even in attribution. On the other hand, inscriptions can be studied as examples of writing as such, in terms, for instance, of the possible variations in the forms of individual letters and the laws that govern the relations between them, and such palacographic analysis gives further welcome aid in dating and attribution.[9]

Moreover, calligraphy in Persia since the medieval times has had a profound, not to say the controlling influence on other arts; providing indispensable discipline as well as concrete ideal for the painter, illuminator and designer and forming all the principal substance of the architectural ornament. Mostly all the great Persian artists have been practising the art of calligraphy in one way or the other. In reality, "Writing seems the direct expression of the spirit of man, and to the mystic the immediate translation of the vision, of the Ultimate, without the intervention of the objective facts that the illustrator must use."[10] In this field of creative art man feels himself spiritually involved: "Calligraphy may be able or skilful, but this is faint praise; in the next category above it is wonderful; but the brush strokes of the supreme calligraphers are divine, and divine in the specific sense that they penetrate the Highest Being."[11]

Under the teachings of Islam, Muslim artists were (and still are) stimulated to excel themselves in all the arts — minor or plastic. By employing their mastery over the discipline of writing, particularly beautifying the Word of *'Allah',* they created different forms and patterns. These include *Mail, Mashq, Kufic, Naskh, Rehān, Sulus, Muhaqqiq, Riqa, Tauqi, Ghubar, Dīwānī, Maghribi, Bihar, Gulzar, Tāj and Nasta'alīq*.[12] Muslim calligraphists, by using these different scripts produced the Qur'anic Verses and other spiritual poetry with commendable lucidity. **(See Plate 2, 3, 4, 20, 28, 30).**

The earliest reference to the Arabic script proper is with the name *Jazm* and it is said that several calligraphic Variants were developed from this script. Each was being called by a name relating to its particular lacality, such as the *Ambari* of Ambar, the *Hiri* of Hirah, the *Makki* of Meccah and the *Madani* of Medinah.[13] But these different names did not imply that the variants had developed very distinctive charactertistics. There were two important scripts---one was cursive and easy to write called *Muqawwar* (rounded), and an other called *Mabsut* (angular). Muslim scholar-artists believe that these two main styles gave birth of all other subsequent scripts and Hijaz and Kufah were the prime centres for some important forms of Islamic calligraphy :

> Only two styles were maintained, each with distinct features; one was cursive and easy to write, called *Muqawwar*, and the other, called *Mabsut*, was angular and consisted to thick straight strokes

> forming rectilinear characters. These two main features governed the development of the early Meccan-Medinan scripts, and led to the formation of a few styles, the most important of which were *Ma'il* (slanting), *Mashq* (extended) and *Naskh* (inscriptional). It is interesting to note that these three styles were current in Hijaz when Kufic script was being developed in Kufah, and endured until after the major reform of the Arabic scripts which was carried out in that city. The *Mashq* and *Naskh* continued to be used after considerable improvements, whereas the Ma'il was discontinued, being replaced by the monumental and hieratic Kufic.[14]

Generally, the art of calligraphy or artistic writings can be divided into two principal styles: (1) the *Kūfic*, deriving its very name from Kufah, as mentioned above, and (2) the *Naskh*. The Muslim calligraphers have shown their keen interests in both the styles. The earliest copy of the Holy Book—Qur'ān which has come down to us was written in *Kūfic* script. This peculiar style of calligraphy with angular letters remained popular amongst the Muslim people in general and calligraphists in particular.

After the 5th/11th Century this *Kufic* script gave place everywhere almost invariably to *naskh* with rounded letters in sharp contrast to the angularities of the kufic style. It is firmly believed that "the kufic form of the script emerged as the most important of several variants. It is fairly austere with a low vertical profile and a horizontal emphasis, typically written on oblong or extended rectangular pages and panels".[15]

The Iranian calligraphers demonstrated mostly in 'vertical style' under the Great Saljuqs. The art of calligraphy and illumination found its richness and extremely beautiful state under the Suljuqs. Iranian artists used to follow the third century's great painter — Mani. Thus, the Iranian calligraphers contributed a lot with their overmastering skill to the Arabic script and its different methods of calligraphy :

> In Iran, after the Islamic conquest, the indigenous artists cultivated the scripts adopted by the Arabs and also the methods of illuminations which were then popular in other Muslim countries. The Iranian calligraphers, under the Great Saljuqs, however, generally emphasized in their calligraphy the vertical as distinguished from the horizontal. The type of illumination and calligraphy found under the Saljuqs is varied, rich, and extremely beautiful since the Iranian genius could fall back upon the tradition of Mani. Mani (third century A.D.) himself was reputed as an excellent painter, but this disaples were also well known for beautiful illumination and charming calligraphy. Specimens of the works of Mani's followers have been unearthed in Central Asia in the turfan basin and it has become abundantly clear that the Iranian calligraphists and artists gave free reign to their indigenous genius whill adapting the Arabic script and method of calligraphy.[16]

Generally, it is said that perhaps during the 6th/13th century a new school of writing was developed in Iran which was known as *ta'liq*. The characters of this very type of writing tend to slope downward from right to left. *Ta'liq* form of writing flourished but the *naskh* script also remained in use especially in religious texts. Thus both the types remained in use during and after the above century.

Under the patronage of well-known kings Il-Khans (654-750/1256-1349) of Persia, various art - forms flourished and got due recognition. The art of calligraphy and illumination was executed in a fine manner. Iraian artists with their inherited rich creative artistic heritage produced various illuminated manuscripts and developed the art of calligraphy as a branch of painting at this stage. The abstract ornamental designs and colour-scheme (especially the use of gold and blue) in background made this Iranian art form distinguishable from other arts. In fact, art has its own uniqueness :

> (The) illuminated pages of books were for the first time decorated with abstract ornamental designs. This may have been due to Chinese influence which permeated painting, and since calligraphy was considered to be a branch of painting, it was bound to be affected thereby. The illuminated manuscripts of this period show geometrical compositions of great beauty and charm, the favourite colours being gold and blue. It may be remembered that the use of gold-dust was a peculiar feature of the book illuminations produced by Mani's followers. There is no doubt that the Iranian artists never forget their national heritage and used the background colour--mainly gold and blue--in sharp contrast to other colours in the foreground with great dexterity and sensibility.[17]

Further, it was during the rule of the Timurid kings in Iran that calligraphic art got its full development. As we know, the princes of the House of Timur were very creative, polished diplomats, skilful administrators and celebrated devotees of Fine Arts. It was due to their creative genius that the art of calligraphy underwent a revolutionary change and the composite form *Na'sta'alīq* was invented which is a highly developed type of writing combining the elegance, vigour and charm of both the forms — *Naskh* and *Ta'līq*. It is generally believed that the credit goes to Mir 'Alī of Tabriz as the inventor of this composite form of writing. One of the famous princes of the House of Timur, namely Sultan Hussain is justly celebrated for being one of the greatest patrons of arts and learning. It is rightly stated that Sultan 'Alī Meshedī, the famous calligraphist, was a protege of his. Other famous calligraphers of this period were Jafar of Tabriz, 'Abd al-Karīm, and Sultan Ibrāhīm (son of Shah Rukh). It is said that Sultān Ibrāhīm was most capable and creative and had the ability to write in six different styles. A copy of the Holy Qur'ān written by him in 824/1424 is preserved in the shrine of Imam Rida in Meshed, (Iran).[18]

The Timurid and Safavid rulers patronized both calligraphy and its associated art, painting, and thus calligraphic decoration on the ceramic tiled interiors of Mosques rose to magnificent heights. In the 11th century another elaborate and somewhat personal script called *shikastah* come into use. This romantic hand, blurred the beginnings and endings of words and letters, linking them using all the space available.

In short, the Islamic art of calligraphy developed tremendously under the patronage of Islamic wisdom in Iran. The Holy Qur'ān is the link between the Arabic script and the Islamic world. The Qur'ān when written, assumes an importance of its own. The writing used to record the Words of the Divinity in various forms, and its very use assumes an importance in the religion. With this stimulus or aim, it became essential to use the finest calligraphy that could be achieved using the primitive script. It was Iran which played a significant role in this field. In this connection it would be true to say that the word of (*Allah*) God together with the hand of man combined to create perhaps the greatest examples of calligraphy in the history of mankind. The explosive artistic energy created by this new partnership flowed throughout the world of Islam.[19]

(B) MINIATURE PAINTING :

Iran has long been famous for its architecture, poetry and painting. Since the rise of Islam in Iran in the mid-6th century A.D., when the Arabs converted most Iranians to Islam different art-forms were existing there. Under the influence of Islam, Iranian artists were stimulated to excel themselves in all art-forms. By the mid-8th Century Iran had became a world's great centre of art, literature, *fiqh* and science.

It is said that the Muslim attitude towards painting in the early history of Islam was inimical and negative one. M. Ajmal very briefly gives the reasons why Muslims had this attitude :

> It seems that the Muslim attitude towards painting in the early history of Islam was hostile. This was justifiable because Fine Arts had at that time an uncanny association with pagan beliefs and rituals. Painting was reminiscent of polytheism which Islam had come to fight against and destory. Islam then needed an extraverted attitude an — attitude in which the soft and feminine qualities of artistic creation and appreciation could find little room. The social consciousness of man at that period of history did not have sufficient insight into subtle differentiation of various aspects of life. Being a facet of pagan polytheism painting was prohibited by Islam in its zeal to break idols.[20]

It is fact that there has always been a love - hate relationship between Islam and painting and even today a considerable number of Muslims is against painting. Although closely linked with calligraphy, painting was considered a low and pseudo art and the painter did not rank with the calligrapher. In spite of all this some of the greatest miniature paintings of the world were executed within the confines of the Islamic world and for this art the whole credit goes to Iran.

Islam itself has never sanctioned or sponsored painting, so religious art as such is unknown. This is in marked contrast to Buddism or Hindusim and Christianity—all stimulated vigorous religious represental art in two or three dimensions. But in Islam the position was different. There was no religious or for that matter, public painting in the world of Islam, because painting was a private affair both in execution and appreciation. Mughals in India, under the influence of Iran, contributed much in the art of miniature painting.

There is still confusion regarding Islamic validity and acceptability of painting. There are different stories as well as divergent theological arguments in this regard :

> Over the centuries strong theological arguments have been made against pictorial representation of both animals and humans, in fact of all living creatures. Figurative art was regarded as an encroachment of the prerogative of Allah, an argument twisted and used in favour of painting in India under the Moghuls. Exactly what is allowed under Islam has never really been clear. There are so many conflicting theories. It has been said that a picture is allowed providing it does not portray Allah or the face of the Prophet. Sculpture, on the other hand, is only permitted if it portrays a stylised animal. There is a story which describes how the Prophet caused the destruction of all states and murals in the Qa'aba sparing only a figure of the Virgin and child. The theological arguments probably arose from the fact that in Arabia, the birth place of Islam, there was no pictorial tradition. Also, from the fact that there was no religious necessity for religious representational art, its place being filled by calligraphy renderings of the word of God from the Koran (Qur'ān). However, there have always been theological disputes as to whether or not painting was prohibited by the Prophet. The dilemma of representational art runs throughout the history of Islam.[21]

But it is clear that there were profound aesthetic possibilities inherent in Islam and these had been realized when the human consciousness developed with a view to foster and nourish so that man could become master of his history and responsible for its vicissitudes. Once this attitude was fairly established in their history, the Muslims began to pay attention to those pagan pursuits (such as painting) which they had neglected before and which were now shorn of their polytheistic associations. Now Muslim artists tried to make their painting as representing *Allah's* creatures and imitating His Creative Power with a view to come nearer or to Him :

> Painting was no longer the art of making images but the art of breaking images. Through painting one could now cast out the devils of one's heart and thus prepare one's soul for direct encounter with God. There was no longer any question of worshipping the gods one painted, for no longer did they remain the objects of worship for the Muslim mind.[22]

Miniature painting became a distinctive feature in Iranian art in particular and Islamic art-world in general. Iranian miniature paintings especially — the Mongol style under the Il-Khans, Shiraz and the Iranian tradition in the 14th century; art under the Timurids (1400-1450); the Shiraz school style from 1415 to 1503; the Herat school of painting (1452-1510); the Safavi school under Shah Tahmasp; the styles of --the Bukhara and other Provincial schools and the later Safavi painting (till 1697)[23] have their remarkable place and importance in the history of painting-world.

The orientalists have always seen and interpreted Islamic art and thought through their narrow and one-sided out-look. They say that all Muslim philosophy and art emerged under the influences of various other non-Islamic cultures and traditions. They maintain that there was nothing original in Islamic art. This view of the orientalists is wrong because they do not see that Islam itself propogates the importance of 'reason' and 'action', 'free will' and 'creativity'. They fail to realize that Islam not only absorbed external influences but also modified them to suit its own native genius. Islam deals with every aspect of human life. Muslim painting was only an aspect of Muslim life. In reality, it was an expression of the spiritual explorations of sensitive minds. Islamic art is the outcome of spiritually - oriented feelings of the creative and penetrative minds :

> These sensitive minds, rooted in their own culture, had their own peculiar longings and yearnings, aspirations, and conflicts. It was out of these dynamic forces that peculiar idioms and patterns of artistic expression were evolved. It is these idioms and patterns which we call by the name of Muslim art.[24]

Muslim painting, especially the miniature painting in Iran, was solely devoted to represent mystical states. Every painting was created in a natural atmosphere. The mystical and pantheistic tendencies of the Persian painters have clearly reflected from their paintings. The trees, flowers, birds, animals etc.. were given in painting to express artists' deep emotional attachment with nature. They regarded every object of nature as the manifestation of God (*Allah*). At every moment new world emerges and therefore, for a Muslim artist simultaneity of eternity is for more important than succession of events. This aspect is unique in Persian miniature painting :

> Muslim painting, especially in Iran, was devoted to the expression of a single emotion in one painting. Every detail of the subject

> was perceived and made use of for an effective rendering of the subtle nuances of that emotion. The trees and flowers were not there to fill a background; they were there to add to the melody flowing from a painting. Most of the Persian miniature paintings are like orchestras in which each object painted contributes to the symphony. This unique characteristic of Muslim painting may have emanated -- as Basil Gray suggests--from the mystical and pantheistic tendencies of the Persians; they, perhaps, regarded every object of nature as manifesting God. But a more plausible explanation of this singular quality can, perhaps, be found in the Muslim conception of time. Muslims regard duration as continuous and eternal, time as discontinuous; universe for them is new at each moment. One continuously hears the sound of *Kun fa-yakūn*. For a Muslim artist, therefore, simultaneity of eternity is far more significant than succession of events. The emotional meaning of an object is implicitly contained in the total situation.[25]

The central theme in the Iranian miniature painting has been Divine. Since each moment is an act of *Allah*, the Muslim painter sees every temporal and spatial situation as somehow transcending serial time and geometrical space. The painter's peculiar perception gives a painting its particular individuality and uniqueness. But the fact is that this array of objects in reality, is the manifestation of the divine which gives it an aura of universality. It would be right to say that both particularity and universality are in reality, combined and synthesized in a single work of miniature art. The entire work of art has emanated from the 'mystical' tendencies of the Persians: "The central position of this cycle in the history of Persian painting follows from the aniconic character of the Islamic religion...."[26] The art of Muslim miniature painting is grounded in the literary and religious texts. In reality, all Muslim paintings, especially miniatures, are illustrations of literary and religious classics such as Niẓami's *Khamsa*, Sa'adi *Gulistān* (moral tales) and *Bostān*, Ḥafiz's *Dīwān*, Jāmī's *Baharistān* and al-*Tawarikh*, Hariri's *Maqaniat*, Firdawsi's *Shah-Nāmah* (book of the kings), *Kalīla wa Dimna*, (Album from the Imperial Palace of Yildiz), *Ẓafar Nāmah* (Life of Timur), *Qiṣaṣ al-Anbiyā'* of Nishapuri, *Hamzanamah* etc. etc. These are some of the most important works to be mentioned in the context of Muslim miniature painting. In almost all the illustrations the depiction of natural objects seems an essential part of the miniature painting. It is so because a Muslim artist firmly believes that nature itself is the Sign of *Allah*. The words of the Holy Qur'ān are the source of communication with God and thus the 'Word' for a Muslim has a compelling power of creation as the spirit must fly to Eternity on the wings of Words. Hence every sensuous experience which inspires a painter to express his inner self--in colour and line--in order to be integrated in his personality, must be capable of verbal expression :

> Muslim paintings—again especially miniatures — are illustrations of literary and religious classics. Several explanations of this peculiar characteristic have been advanced. But the only explanation which is consistent with the general Muslim attitude is that for a Muslim nature is itself an illustration of the Word of God. *Kun fa-yakūn* are the words which translate themselves into the sensible world. The world is Logos in matter and motion. Muslim consciousness is rooted in the awareness of a profound interrelationship between word and fact. Word seems to be the life-blood of the universe.[27]

The art of miniature painting became a significant feature of Iranian art in particular and Islamic art-world in general. Muslim painting, especially in Iran, was solely devoted to Divinity. *Allah* is the source of everything and, therefore, the Iranians regarded every object of nature as manifestation of God. It is due to this fact that we find the elements of nature in every Iranian miniature painting. The Iranian artists were much inspired by nature and their approach to art was mystical one.

(C) DECORATIVE ARTS :

Iran has been famous for its arts, architecture and civilization. Iranian artists and architects won name and fame in every field of life. Their contribution, especially in the fields of architecture and decorative arts, deserve special appreciation in the Islamic art-world. In the following pages we shall briefly discuss minor or decorative arts one by one in order to highlight the creative potentiality as well as aesthetic sensibility of Iranian artists. Though we have already given a short account of these arts in the Introductory Chapter of this project, yet some more areas still require to be considered in addition to them.

(1) Designs in Decorating Buildings :

Iranian architects designed and built magnificent Mosques, Madrasa as and Palaces. They had excellent innovative power to create different designs for the decoration of these buildings including their own homes. They decorated the walls. roofs or domes, ceilings etc. with brightly coloured mosaic and tile designs.

The architectural decoration has become the unique artistic achievement of the Persian artists. The decorative enrichment of the Persian architecture is the remarkable distinction in the field of world-architecture :

> Architectural decoration has often been adjudged Persia's most notable artistic achievement. The inventive powers of Persian designers through all ages generated a profusion of patterns based a few fundamental themes which were remarkably vital and prolific. Old techniques of ornamentation were continued over long periods, while new ones were continuously developed with ever-increasing refinement, and all were carried to a degree of perfection that was probably not equalled elsewhere. This virtuousity supplied the architects with an immense repertoire of ornament which was admirably adapted to the enrichment of the large masses and palin surfaces characteristic of Persian building.[28]

i) **Geometrical Designs** :

Geometry became highly important element in the Islamic world of art. Its figures and constructions were permeated with symbolic, cosmological significance. In different Islamic designs 'geometry' became an essential part and acquired metaphysical and religious significance. While decorating buildings Muslim artists mostly used geometry based designs :

> In architecture strict adherence to geometric principles in plans and elevations was the basis of the harmony and discipline which characterise all Islamic art. In decoration geometrically-based designs covered entire surfaces, typically with a geometrical framework leaving spaces to be filled with interlaced and stylised leaf and floral designs... The close association between geometry, cosmology and symbolism has led some scholars ... to read metaphysical and religious significance into the geometrical content of both finished designs and the postulated grids on which the designs must have based.... While it is probable that geometrical designs were not seen merely as abstract patterns but as imbued with a sacred content [particularly in religious contexts],

> it seems unlikely that the carftsman decorating a wall or carving a door would have had these properties uppermost in his mind. Rather he would be following the teaching of his master and the traditional skills of his craft, and he would no a doubt have left to others the philosophical interpretations of the traditional patterns he produced.[29]
> (Please See Plate **23** , **25**).

Muslim designers, especially Iranians say that geometry-based designs help the craftworker to maintain equal proportion and decency in decorating buildings or illumination. Such designs can be enlarged or reduced on the basis of the proportional relationships between geometrical figures. These designs can easily be repeated and, with the help of addition of straight and curved lines, changed in limitless other designs :

> Geometrical designs are basically very simple they may be constructed with only a compass and a rule and the knowledge of certain procedures which produce traingles, squares, hexagons, stars, etc. The designs may be reduced and enlarged with great case. By repeating these procedures, and through further division and the addition of straight and curved lines, almost limitless elaboration variations may be achieved.′Once the grid has been laid down there is scope for individual experimentation. Although these designs often appear highly complex there are no mysteries; all that is needed is a logical approach and a steady hand and nerve. The best way to understand the geometrical patterns is to draw them.[30]

ii) <u>Carved and Molded Plaster Designs</u> :

Muslim artists decorated buildings from Spain to Turkestan with molded plaster medium. Iranian craftworkers designed floral arabesques and large letters in wet plaster on walls and arches. In decorating walls and ceilings Iranian artists used geometric ornaments and inscriptions, all molded in stucco and painted or gilded. Geometrical designs were executed in the molded plaster medium.

The best example of stucco relief designs can be seen in *Masjid-i-Jāmi* (in Shiraz). We find that during the first centuries in the Islamic architectural ornoment in Persia, the 'stucco' was the best medium and this pattern provided a distinctive feature in Persian architectural - world. In this connection Arthur Upham Pope has rightly remarked :

> The *Masjid-i-Jāmi* of Shiraz, hidden under the soffit of the arch in front of the badly damaged *miḥrāb*, which cannot be later than about 894, is a strip of superb stucco relief ornament which even now retains some of its original background colour, and an examination of the face of the arch shows that this was originally covered with a similar decoration.
> Executed in hard, fine-grained stucco, this scrolling foliate stem between pearled bands winds and flutters with enchanting grace. The pattern, 'which stands halfway between designs in the Dome of the Rock and certain motifs in the stucco of Nayin,' has been accounted by some one of the masterpieces of Persian stucco ornament; but while its merits as a design are incontestable, its fitness as architectural ornament is not so certain. The fluidity and liveliness of movement imported by the swiftly sweeping spirals, marks of its superiority as pattern, are not altogether appropriate to a structural unit that requires strength and stability, and the design on the face was, if anything, more emphatic and proportionately less adopted to its architectural emplacement. Moreover, in its original condition the discrepancy was even more market, for the background was dark blue, against which the sharp white lines of the relief stood out with a lace-like transparency, more suggestive of a void beyond than of the solid stones of the arch that surtains the weight above.[31]

iii) <u>The Leaf Scroll Motif</u> :

In Iranian decorative art-forms the leaf scroll become a most versatile decorative motif. In every field (be it building decoration, textile, book - illumination etc.) we find this as one of the world's most popular and enduring motifs. Together with the plaited and interlaced borders, frames and knots and key patterns, which are also motifs of the ancient ancestry and enduring popularity, the palmetto flower and scroll are among the handful of decorative devices in Iranian fine arts and which yet seem never to go out of fashion. We see many textile and wall-paper designs today featuring one or the other of these motifs.

We also find leaf scroll motif in stucco relief in different religious and public buildings. The stucco ornament became the central element of a attraction in Iranian architecture' for example, in Isfahan and Gulpayagan we see other motifs such as brick end and terra-cotta, but the stucco device was considered important in decorating buildings. The stucco relief pattern has its own decorative value :

> In the Great Dome Chamber at Isfahan, for example, the spandrels in the transition zone were all originally decorated with a framework of thick stemmed arabesques, that, as we know from the similar patterns on the *Ivan* vault of the Ardistan Masjid-i-Jami, are impressive at a considerable distance; and traces of similar work are discernible in the spandrels of the arches in the Gulpayagan Masjid-i-Jami. But the stucco designer still played a subordinate role, for in both Isfahan and Gulpayagan the principal surfaces are primarily of exposed brick and the supplementary plaster or terracotta ornament is restricted to such fine patterns as to be, in their present condition at least, scarcely visible. This old technique of carved terracotta fillings inserted in the interestices of a geometrical framework in plain brick did, no doubt, give a rich texture to the whole interior, but it was, unless brightly poly-chromed (a rather doubtful assumption), of little decorative

value. The need for more impressive and more structural forms that should harmonize with the grandeur of the great domes was gratified at Isfahan in part by the superb trilobe squinch and in Gulpayagan by filling the squinches with powerful brick stalactite clusters, supplemented with round plaques in the spandrels. But the plasterer continued his gradual intrusion into the field of organmental brickwork.[32]

The other examples of stucco design are *Masjid-i-Ḥydaria* (in Qazvin), *Masjid-i-Jāmī* (Nayin), and *Masjid-i-Jāmī* (Varamin), Tomb of 'Alī ibn-Abī Ma'alī (Qumm); in all these religious buildings especially stucco relief *Miḥrabs* and calligraphy as well as minor borders from stucco decoration are important to be referred here.

Thus, the Iranian craft-men or artists created different patterns or art-motifs as well as versatile decorative designs for their architectural world. They were really masters in the field of architectural ornament. In decorating **walls, roofs,ceilings, tombs, *meḥrābs*** etc. they used mostly geometrical designs, carved and molded plaster designs, terro-catta and brick-end designs.

(2) The Ceramic Arts :

Like other different art forms, Iran has long been famous for its beautiful Ceramic art. Iranian craft-workers have been making beautiful jewelery, metelware and pottery. The ceramic art reached its highest development between the 8th century and 13th century A.D.[33]

Pottery furnishes perhaps the most comprehensive record of the artistic life and aesthetic feeling of Islamic Persia. We find that other arts have also been equally significant for many periods. But, as mentioned above, since eighth century onwards, "We have for each successive era masses of pottery in a steadily expanding series, representing numerous styles and techniques, and illustrating nearly every phase of the Persian artistic consciousness".[34] Generally it is said that pottery is the excellent manifestation of the Islamic Persian aesthetic genius.

The Persian Ceramic art was the result of the deep aesthetic sensibility of Persian designers. They decorated pottery in a number of different patterns, such as; miniature figures of birds or animals, men or women of various professions, folk-lore and literature, scenes from the Court and from ordinary life of people etc. In this connection A.U. Pope writes :

> It is also, perhaps, the most characteristic. It gave direct and sensitive expression to artistic feeling. In its graceful shapes Persian ideas of form found their most immediate and perfect embodiment. The subtly toned glazes which the ceramists had mastered by the early medieval period probably contributed directly to the distinguished colour sense that found magnificent fulfillment in the carpets, textiles, and painting of the Safavid period. Designers and painters had been called into service at a date well prior to any surviving miniatures, and the decoration of certain early wares shows draftsmanship of a high order that throws indispensable light, not only on ornament, but also on the evolution of Persian painting. Even the beginning of an interest in sculpture is evident in some types of relief decoration, and quite a number of figures in the round were attempted. Many pieces depict, too, textile patterns, costume, furniture, the dance, and even, though sketchily, architecture. Folk-lore and literature, scenes from the Court and from ordinary life, sober designs and fantastic invention, all are represented. The character of each epoch as well as the deeper cultural trends that were fashioning Persian life both find expression and record in pottery.[34]

(i) The Importance of Ceramics in Persian Art :

The art of pottery has very important place in Persian aesthetic world. Its importance has been underlined by various reasons. Arthur Upham Pope in this connection mentions that one reason why the Pottery of Persia is such a comprehensive record of Persian art is that it was so intimately associated with the very life of the people. The pottery functioned in life at every turn and it was as useful and natural to the Persian people as their garments.

There are a variety of forms of pottery. Persian people have many kinds of pottery in their daily use and display. Through this variety we can understand their creative and aesthetic sensibility. Arthur Pope mentions a long list of this variety of pottery with reference to Umar Khayyam :

> The variety of forms and uses is all but infinite. We have beakers and goblets, plasks, bottles, ewers, jugs, rose-water sprinklers, aquamaniles, bowls, plates, deep dishes, platters, basins, trays, sweetmeat compartment trays, compotiers; jars of all sizes, from tiny cosmetic containers to storage jars for wine oil, butter, or wheat, sometimes large enough to hold at least one of the Forty Thiever; pen.boxes, though these are rare; ink wells, spittoons, money containers, boxes for scales, multiple-spouted flower holders, candlesticks, lanterns, bird-houses, incense-burners, qalyans (waterpipe bowls), foot rests, Kashkuls (beggars' bowls), magic bowls with protective signsand inscriptions, rubbing stones and bread stamps with faience grips, cup holders, labourettes, and braziers, while Umar Khayyam is credited with the invention of caly scarecrows. an odd task for the ceramist; nor does this exhaust the list, for in Persia the pottery quite surpassed the ordinary limits of his craft. His art became the handmaiden of architectures supplying not merely dadoes, mouldings, cornices, window-frames and grills, and the great *Miḥrābs*, but even providing tile and mosaic revetments that covered entire buildings, which for sheer magnificence of colour and pattern have never been equalled.[36]

On the vessels different aspects of life have been portrayed due to which this ceramic art added more depth and artistic enrichment to Iranian art. Vessels were also made for delight and contemplation, often too fragile to be safely used; others richly embossed and gilded, could not long have withstood any but the gentlest use. Utility may have been an excuse, but beauty was their reason and purpose. On the vessels decorative sculptural pieces include a variety of human figures and quite a range of simply drawn animals, landscapes etc.

The essential quality of Persian Pottery is best appreciated by comparing it with the ceramic arts of Greece and China. It is observed that Greek pottery is often assumed to be the utmost achievement of the potter's art, and it is true that the finest examples are, in reality, superb. But from the ceramic point of view Greek pottery is not altogether sound and it is , as Arther Pope believes, distinctly meagre. No variety of colour scheme is there in the Greek art of pottery. Persian Pottery, on the other hand, has in it a cultural representation and it has its ceramic character too. There is a variety of colours used in this art. Similarly, the Chinese ideal does not have that very depth and artistic uniqueness which the Persian pottery has. The ceramic art of Persia has other different ideals and by them it must be judged and appreicated.

Distinguishing the art of Persian pottery from the Chinese one Arthur Pope writes that the ideal of Chinese potter or Ceramic designer is different from that of the Persian one. The Persian potter has rich spiritual imagination and literary taste and the same ideal has been realized or materialized in the ceramic art :

> We find little of the self-conscious virtuosity by which the Chinese potter, torturing his simple clay into novel and inappropriate forms, sometimes demonstrated his skill by outraging the substance which he was bound to be treat with respect. For the Persian potter the clay was almost like a companion or colleague, and to it he devoted the imagination of a poet, the sensitive rhythm of a dancer, the quick and graceful finger of the trained calligrapher, and withal an implied philosophy that saw and felt in common substances nothing alien and opaque, but something near and friendly, which, under guidance, might reveal its own destiny and become a fellow witness to the beauty that is imprisoned in all existence. Not many potters would probably thus have formulated their creed, although a zest for poetry and philosophy has for centuries characterized all classes in Persia, and Sufism made vocal this implicit idea; but practice as well as words can express a conviction, and it was this attitude towards matter in itself which determined their ideal as potters, leading them to seek, not the final concealment, but the realization of the quality and 'intentions' of the material.[37]

Islamic art has its spiritual significance. *Allah* is the source of every art and though in Islamic *Weltanschauung*. Art and beauty is not luxury as some Muslims and Western historians of art consider, but in reality, Islam considers beauty to be a Divine quality and teaches that God loves beauty.[38] Therefore, the Muslim artists or craft-workers, especially the Iranians, tried to create every form of art under the spiritual inspiration. The ceramic art comes first of its kind in which we find that Iranian craftworkers used and infused in it metaphysical and cosmological significance. Thus innumberable qualities "have emerged from Islamic spirituality and have manifested themselves over the ages in many different climes in the various traditional arts of Islam from *pottery* to literature and music".[38]

(ii) Colour, Design and Subject-Matter :

The Iranian artists have their distinctive colour scheme that can easily discerned. In the ceramic art they developed or created an astonishing variety of sumptuous colours. Aestheticians of different fields of art do consider that it is this best colour arrangement that is the cause for the chief glory of Persian pottery.

Iranian potters have a consistent quality of their own and their colour-scheme in the field of ceramic art is somewhat different from those colour compositions of textiles or carpets. Briefly, it can be noticed that the Iranian craftworker uses blues, greens, yellows, golds, blacks, reds, creams and maroons and clay pigments etc. in his ceramic art. Some of these colours are used just for outlines or for charming effects. Arthur Upham Pope beautifully explains the ceramic colour-scheme in the following words :

> A clear and intense turquoise is the dominant tone in the monochrome group, but a deep lapis lazuli blue is only a little less favoured, and finally a cobalt glaze is perfected which is unmatched for its intensity, while a pale blue that sinks into the glaze permits some charming effects. Greens are less common, but for some wares and periods are of striking beauty. The emerald green of the Garrus pottery at its best will bear any comparison, and the pale green of some of the painted enamel wares, a rare colour, is delightfully set off by pure gold. The palette was extended with aubergine; various cream colours, occasionally attaining a beautiful yellow, a fluctuating maroon which is used for enrichment; and black for accents, while dark

> tones are sometimes overpainted with touches of white that freshen them like cool spray. The full expansion of the colour range came with the application of enamels and the development and use of clay pigments which brought to these subtle artists a wide selection of new tones. Gold was also used, sometimes treated like a pigment, but in other cases applied in glowing little flecks. A pale red was developed for outlines, and a rose tone also is to be found, though only very rarely. The early Samarqand ceramists made effective use of a sort of cinnabar shade which was set off by white or velvety black, and a fluctuating maroon is important in the painted enamel wares, while in the 'Kubachi' and Sava faience one finds a dull red.[40]

In short, the Iranian artist in the ceramic field created or discovered an exceptional number of ways to ornament their wares or products and his colour compositions play an important role in it. By the discovery of luster painting, and some more daring combinations in the 16th and 17th centuries, this the art of pottery has acquired great importance and received deep appreciation :

> The colour range was greatly enriched by the discovery of lustre painting. Used for the most part in combination with white, the lustre runs into a long series of variations on the fundamental tone of gold now : dark brownish, buff or chamois, now lemon yellow, olive, or sometimes deep carmine, ruby, or garnet, these surfaces flash an endless series of lambent tones that seem to be one dimension beyond colour, as if sunlight itself were caught, imprisoned, and artfully released. More daring combinations were tried in the sixteenth and seventeenth centuries, with burnished copper against a background of cream colour, pale Nile green or light lavender blue.[41]

The Persian ceramists created simple and complex attractive designs for their pottery. They discovered different devices to impart a texture to the surface so that they can ornament their wares in a best manner. Generally, ceramic designs consist of interlacing arcs, circles, geometrical lay-outs and complicated stellate systems. Different kinds of animals, birds, trees, flowers and other natural objects were executed in different ceramic compositions. Each design is thoroughly planned. In the 16th century (A.D.) we also find some poetic creations besides natural and animal life :

> By the sixteenth century, familiarity with the painter's point of view had introduced a landscape conception, and compositions of trees, flowers, and animals are naturalistically conceived as growing up from the ground. The basal systems which govern Persian ceramic ornamentation, although often inconspicuous, are usually essential to the effect. Frequently they impart lucidity and control to the richest inventions, furnishing sound logic for charming poetic creations.[42]

One most important design-technique namely '*alkaline glaze*' was invented in Kashan (Iran), which allowed fine painting to be carried out directly on the surface of the frit body and covered with a transparent glaze without the colours spreading into the glaze during firing. This became a famous technique in Kashan and combined with the use of cobalt blue was adopted by the Chinese in the fourteenth century :

> For a short period in the early 13th century the 'water weed' design become a popular motif in Kashan, Iran. The discovery of a clear alkaline glaze, which allowed painting directly on the white frit ware without the colours spreading during firing. made it possible to produce such elegant designs.[43]
> (Please See Plate **22, 25, 27, 29**).

Although this motif sometimes occurs together with fishes. it is unlikely that it represents any particular aquatic plant. These unique designs conform to the traditional scroll form or are arranged with stylized symmetry. We see that shoals of fish decorate the inside of many metal or pottery bowls, often in a rotating design (See Plate 31).

So far as the *subject-matter* or theme of the Persian pottery is concerned it can briefly be said that on the one hand the nature and animal life, and on the other important scenes from human day to day life were the main themes of this form of art :

> The ceramic art was thus maintained in the most natural way by daily use and lively appreciation. It was not created for the special patron, but rather was the spontaneous expression of the needs and taste of a sophisticated public. To be in intimate daily contact with the life of the people and in constant practical use is an advantage to any art. Such a dependence gives art sanity and soundness. and brings to bear upon all its inventions the interment character of the race, its ideals and special genius.[44]

Moreover, for the Persian potter-artist the 'contour' has an identity with reality and the crafworker more or less clearly realizes it and materializes the same with 'clay' (stuff). It is clay which transfers the 'ideal' into 'real'. Again, at the same time. it is believed that clay itself became a theme and various modulations proclaim its character.[45]

In the most of the pottery designs we find that animals of hunt are represented in a conventionalised naturalistic style in the classical tradition. It shows Iranian love for nature as well as for animals.[46]

Though animal life has been the dominant theme of Persian artists. yet the subjects of the personanage designs, apparently royal figures, are also there. We also find other court scenes, incidents from *Shah-Nāmah* and simple scenes occupy the attention and attraction of medieval artists.

Furthermore, the art of *calligraphy* has also been one of the most important themes in the Persian Ceramic world. In every sphere of pottery designs, the treatment is decorative and the beauty of colour and technique is given great importance .

Throughout the first and second periods, we find that calligraphy is an important theme, and the faience inscriptions, incised, or moulded in high relief, or just painted, sometimes vie in beauty with the calligraphy of the Holy Qur'ān. But whatever the theme may be for the Iranian artists, the treatment is always decorative and the beauty of colour and pattern is in most cases the real subject.[47]

(3) SOME OTHER FORMS OF DECORATIVE ART :

In Iran there are some *other important forms of decorative art* such as **rugs** or **carpet**, **textiles**, **metalware**, **glassware**, **calligraphy**, **wood-carving**, **book-illustration**, **book-illumination** and **book-binding**. We have already discussed briefly most of them in the *First Chapter* of this project so there is no need to discuss them again. Briefly, we can say that the Iranian craftworkers make beautiful **jewelry**, **pottery** and **metalware**. Their handwoven Persian **rugs** are prized and appreciated throughout the world for their graceful patterns and soft colours. The complicated designs of the rugs often require months of labour to complete. Other traditional decorative arts in Iran include **embroidery**, **silkweaving**, **woodcarving**, **book-illumination** and **calligraphy**. Iranian architects and designers decorated the walls and domes with brightly coloured mosaic and tile designs. Traditional Persian painting features delicate detail work and jewel-like colours. It is their greatness that they did their best in every form of art and contributed a lot in the field of aesthetics.

REFERENCES

1. *The Holy Qur'ān, op.cit.*, Surah 96:1,3 and 4,5.
2. *Ibid.*, Surah 68: 1.
3. Nasr, S.H., *Islamic Art and Spirituality, op.cit.*, p. 25
4. *Ibid.*, pp. 25-6.
5. *Al-Qur'ān;* Surah 31:27.
6. *cf. The Holy Qur'ān* (Text, Translation & Commentory by Abdullah Yusuf 'Ali), *op.cit.*, p. 1087.
7. Nasr, S.H.. *Islamic Art and Spirituality, op.cit.*, p.18.
8. Pope A.U. & Ackerman P., (editors), *A Survey of Persian Art*, Manafzadeh Group, Tehran./Oxford University Press, London, p. 1707.
9. *Ibid.*, p. 1707.
10. *Ibid.*, p. 1708.
11. *Ibid.*, p. 1708.
12. Aftab Ahmad, *Islamic Calligraphy* (Noon-Wal-Qalam), (Tr. Sajjad Haider Malik), Rajput Printers, Rawalpindi, Pakistan, p. 7, (*Preface*).
13. Safadi, Y.H., *Islamic Calligraphy*, Thames and Hudson Ltd. London. 1978, p. 8.

14. *Ibid.*, p. 9.

15. Wilson, E., *op.cit.*, p. 11.

16. Sharif, M.M., *A History of Muslim Philosophy*, (Vol. II), *op.cit.*, p. 1181.

17. *Ibid.*, p. 1181.

18. *Ibid.*, pp. 1181-2.

19. Bamborough, P., *Treasures of Islam. op.cit.*, pp. 24-5.

20. M. Ajamal, "Painting" in M.M. Sharif's (edt.) *A History of Muslim Philosophy, op.cit.*, p. 1110.

21. Bamborough, P., *op.cit.*, p. 42.

22. Sharif, M.M., *op.cit.*, pp. 1110-1.

23. Gray, Basil, *Persian Painting*, Macmillan London Ltd., London and Basingstoke, 1977, pp. 9-15.

24. Sharif, M.M., *op.cit.*, p. 1111.

25. *Ibid.*, p. 1114.

26. Gray, B., *op.cit.*, p. 12.

27. Sharif, M.M., *op.cit.*, p. 1115.

28. Pope, A.U., & Ackerman, P., *op.cit.*, p. 1258.

29. Wilson, E., *op.cit.*, pp. 14-5.

30. *Ibid.*, p. 15.

31. Pope, A.U., & Ackerman, P., *op.cit.*, pp. 1264-5.

32. *Ibid.*, p. 1293.

33. *The World Book Encyclopedia, op.cit.*, p. 470.

34. Pope, A.U., *op.cit.*, p. 1447.

35. *Ibid.*, p. 1447.

36. *Ibid.*, pp. 1447-8.

37. *Ibid.*, p. 1451.

38. Nasr, S.H., *Islamic Art and Spirituality, op.cit.*, p. 197.

39. *Ibid.*, p. 201.

40. Pope, A.U., *op.cit.*, p. 1453.

41. *Ibid.*, pp. 1453-4.

42. *Ibid.*, p. 1455.

43. Wilson, E., *op.cit.*, p. 74.

44. Pope, A.U., *op.cit.*, p. 1448.

45. *Ibid.*, p. 1456.

46. Wilson, E., *op.cit.*, p. 11.

47. Pope, A.U., *op.cit.*, p. 1458.

CHAPTER IV

MAIN SCHOOLS OF IRANIAN PAINTING

(A) Shiraz School
(B) Herat School
(C) Tabriz School
(D) Qazvin School
(E) Isfahan School

CHAPTER - IV

SCHOOLS OF IRANIAN PAINTING

Generally, painting in the Muslim world has always been associated with the main centres of political power and was largely dependent upon the personal patronage of the rulers or the dignitaries of the state. In the Islamic aesthetic-world 'the art of painting' has a specific background. It was at the court of the Shahs of Iran and India, and Sultans of the Western lands and of Turkey that the great schools of painting flourished in a successful manner. At the same-time it has also been noticed that painting seems almost always to have suffered when royal support was either lacking or withdrawn.

The history of Muslim painting in general and Iranian in particular is closely related to the political history of the Muslim-world and to the fates of the dynasties, courts and cities. Different styles and techniques developed and disappeared with the development and decline of a school of art.

Highlighting and recognising the special position of painting in the Muslim-world, particularly in Iran, scholar-artists have devoted themselves, on the basis of styles, techniques and material, to identify the various court-schools and establish their chronology as well as credibility.

There are various big and small schools of Iranian painting, but we shall briefly discuss some *main* schools here :

(A) SHIRAZ SCHOOL OF IRANIAN PAINTING

Shiraz was very old centre for Iranian culture and art-tradition. It was the capital of southern province for Fars which had been the heart of the Achaemenid Empire. All older traditions of Persian painting flourished more vigorously under this centre. Shiraz was, in reality, founded by the Saffarid and Buwayhid during 9th and 10th centuries respectively, and under the Mongols it became a more prosperous centre with a great Iranian cultural tradition. It was the home-town of famous Persian poets-Sa'adī and Ḥafiz. Shiraz was invaded by Timur in 1393 who revived the art-culture tradition of Persia. Though there were much political ups and downs during the 14th century in Shiraz but even then art-activities—especially the tradition of book-illustration--appeared to have been in progress. Basil Gray writes in this connection :

> Shiraz itself was a creation of the Saffarid (867-900) and Buwayhid (933-1056) dynasties, and under the Mongols was a prosperous city with a great cultural tradition, having been the home of the poet Sa'adi, who died there in 1294, and then of Hafiz, who survived to see the conquest to Timur and died in 1389. But in politics it suffered many violent changes during the century. The house of Inju, descended from the last governor under the Il-Khans, who became independent after the death of Abu Sa'id in 1335, ruled Fars from that date until 1353, when they were ousted by the house of Muzaffar, who had been the rulers of Yazd meanwhile. They had a greater dominion over all south-west Persia until they were finally extirpated by Timur in 1393. Both Abu Ishaq the Inju and Shah Shuja' the Muzaffarid were patrons of Hafiz and might have been expected to have employed skilled artists of the book. In fact the volumes which can with certainty be assigned to Shiraz at this period all fall within the Inju domination. It is not until the eve of the fall of the city to Timur that there is a book which can be given without doubt to the

> Muzaffarids; but we shall try to bridge this gap. For there appears to have been a continuous tradition of book illustration at Shiraz, which is important just because of that continuity.[1]

Timur was a great lover of arts and his efforts in the field of aesthetics deserve special appreciation. It is said that whenever he conquered a country he would take special care not to kill the artists but to regard and encourage them. He used to take them to Baghdad, where under his patronage they copied and illustrated various Persian manuscripts. But the true artistic greatness was achieved only under the inspiring benevolence of his son Shah Rukh who made Herat his home. Later on, Shah Rukh's sons, Iskandar Sultan and Baysunqur Mirza, founded academies of book-arts with a large staff of artists. Thus both the Sultans became the great patrons of Shiraz and Herat respectively. Briefly we can say that Timur and his descendants were great lovers of art and culture and under their patronage Persian painting reached its zenith :

> Timur and his descendants were great patrons of painting, and under them Persian painting had its finest hour. The classic painting of this period is a pure delight to behold. These miniature "treasures" are master pieces of composition and colour, with a fineness of detail which gives them an air of absolute perfection. The painter was master of everything he beheld, he could do with it what he liked. However, he did not lie, he was truthful to the point of ignoring what he saw only portraying what he knew to be there. Thus illusions have no place in Persian art. Rich decorative detail and naturalism were all important. Some of the finest works were produced in Shiraz under Iskandar-Sultan (died 1414) and in Heart under Baysunqur (died 1433) and Sultan Husain Bayqara (died 1506).[2]

At Shiraz. in the 15th century (especially during the first half), on independent school flourished in which colours were milder and cooler and the style, though not vastly different, was definitely less skilful than that of the school at Herat.[3] Though we don't find much difference of the techniques and styles between these two Timurid schools-Shiraz and Herat-as the latter maintains the themes and motifs of the former :

> No serious attempt has yet been made to distinguish between the work of the two main Timurid schools of the fifteenth century, that of Herat and that of Shiraz. Although we have some manuscripts that can be assigned to one or the other with absolute certainty, the criteria that can be deduced from a careful study of these have not seemed to scholars adequate to justify an attempt to classify the great number of unidentified manuscripts of this period still in existence. Such an undertaking can be only a preliminary essay, which will undoubtedly be subject to a good many subsequent corrections. The Shiraz school can best be defined first, as its connexions with the immediately preceding phase of the art are clearer than are those of the herat school, while the latter, on the contrary, maintains a continuity of development in the following period.[4]

Before 1410 Baghdad and Tabriz were the main centres of Iranian miniature painting, but after that Shiraz and Herat became famous places for this art-activity: "After 1410 A.D. Shiraz and Herat replaced Baghdad and Tabriz as the main centres with the emergence of famous patrons such as Iskandar Sultan and Baysunghur."[5]

MAIN THEMES AND ARTISTS OF SHIRAZ SCHOOL :

As we know in Persian art of painting the same themes recur time and again. Poetry, historical and mythological works were extremely popular. Therefore, themes like Nizami's *Khamsa* (five poems), Firdausi's *Shah Nāmah*; Sa'adī's *Būstān* and *Gulistān*; Jāmī's story of *Yūsuf* and *Zulaīkha*; Timur's *Shahanshāh Nāmah*, Anthology of Iskandar Sultan etc. are illustrated with originality by numberous master painters. We also find the Chinese influence in Shiraz school of Iranian painting. (See Plate 1, 10).

The oldest illustrated manuscript which can be proved to derive from the Shiraz school was the *Shah Nāmah* in Istanbul (in 1370). In the illustrations of this manuscript we find romantic landscape without any figure at all, results a few years later here at Shiraz. Other works in the second half of the 14th century include the illustrations of the poems of Khwaju Kirmānī (1397) a *Shah Nāmah* (1370) written in Shiraz. Ernst Kuhnel explains about figures and natural objects in their background of the *Shah Nāmah* as under :

> The figures show very conventional, oval faces, but rather expressive attitudes. The hilly landscape is partly naturalistic, with scattered shrubs, tufts of grass, and flowers, but on other pages there are fantastic semicircular formations in strange decorative style. This is the only documented example so far known of miniature painting from the period when the art of poetry was flourishing in Shiraz (the great Hafiz died there in 1389 (19 IH.), though book illustration must also have attained a high standard there.[6]

Again, during the first half of the 15th century we find another Anthology of Persian poems made (in 1410) for Iskandar Sultan, son of Shah Rukh and governor of Shiraz. This Anthology of the Sultan represents the complete maturity of the Shiraz school. The text has remarkable aesthetic look :

> The division of the text in this manuscript is interesting. Beside the main text (main) runs a marginal text (*ḥashiya*), with small decorative corners in an arrangement that will be found in other manuscripts of the same type. In some cases the text runs into the illustration, other miniatures are wholly isolated, and several different artists certainly contributed to the volume. Some of the episodes involving mounted men, such as horsemen fighting with lances, or polo games, show, in the skilful grouping, the fresh

> treatment, and the free and inevitable placing of the figures in the landscape, the complete development of the stylistic trend which had already appeared in the Cairo Shah-Nama. The court scenes, on the other hand, though no less attractive in colour, are much more conventional in treatment, with relatively large figures, often in rather stiff poses, and flowering shrubs filling the spaces between them[7].

Further, we have another small Anthology containing principally Nizami's epics which had also been made for Iskandar Sultan in 1410 and rightly considered among the main works of the Shiraz school.

Again, in another Collection of Nizami we find the illustrations of different love-stories like *Khusraw's Struggle with the Lion in front of Shirin's Tent; Shirin's Visit to Farhād; Majnun as a Mendicant in front of Laila's Tant etc.*, which come out of the manuscript in about 1430. Here in these illustrations we observe the tall figures of the women, the ornamentation on the tent, the landscape etc. all of which have appeared already in the other works of this school. Everything has been presented in a beautiful manner here.

The best known work composed and illustrated in Shiraz during Sultan Ibrahim's time was the *Zafar Nāmah* (the life of Timur) by the Master Artist Sharaf al-Din 'Alī Yazdi. It was finished in 1425

We have here, at Shiraz, another richly illustrated copy of the *Shah Namah* dedicated to Sultan Ibrahim in about 1435 in which the simple landscape-background, the high horizon, the vigorous action and the skilful use of simple colours are there. "From a blending of the Muzaffared and early Timurid Court style sprang the court style of Ibrahim."[8] In this connection scenes like

Rustum catching his Horse Rakhsh from the wild Herd and *Landscape with Animals in Gold and Silver* are important to be referred here.[9]

In Shiraz School there is another *Shah Namah* manuscript dated 1444 copied by Muhammad al-Sultani. In these illustrations we find banquet scenes where the action is bold and spacious and the colouring wonderfully rich in range and intensity[10] (See Plate **10**). Basil Gray explains all the particulars in the light of Shiraz School's aesthetic demanstration in the following words :

> Figure drawing, cloud forms and foliage connect them with the Shiraz school, and all the particulars, as well as the size....The right-hand page bears on the reverse an illuminated Shams, unfortunately without the name of the prince for whom it was prepared, filled in; and on the reverse of the left-hand page is the beginning of the Baysunghur preface to the Epic with a good illuminated heading. Although it might be thought that the subject, a royal feast in a garden, would not lend itself to movement, the forceful gesture of a single figure in each half of the double composition and the leaning stance of many of the figures do in fact give a sense of great vegetation and the sumptuous textiles, in which gold and silver are not spared, make the background like a tapestry. Certainly the Timurid school of Shiraz showed no sign of decline in vigour in its last decade.[11]

In the middle and the second half of the 15th century we have seen some important illustrations from *Khāwar Nāmah* of Ibn Husam. We find here in these masterpieces of Shiraz school that the basic Persian inclination to 'symmetry' and 'decoration' is prominent. This aspect is most clearly observed in the richly illustrated manuscript of *Khāwar Nāmah* an epic life of Shia's first Imam 'Ali, the son-in-law of the Prophet Muhammad. It was composed in 1426 and is considered as the last of the imitations of the *Shah Nāmah*. The best examples of this illustrated manuscript are : *Gabriel Shows the Powers of 'Alī to the Prophet Muḥammad* (1480); *'Alī Removes a Pillar Placed by Solomon in a Cave and Releases a Supply of Good Water* (1480) and *Gabriel Announces the Apotheosis of 'Alī* (1480).[12]

CONCLUSION :

To sum up the entire discussion on Shiraz School, we can say that the painting in Shiraz falls into *two* periods: the *first* under the Timurids when the style is close to that of the Herat School and, the *second* a more isolated, independent style in Safavid times. During the first phase certain local differences can be observed; there are fewer but larger figures than at Herat, elongated expressionless, in compositions with a decorative, high horizon with little vegetation except rocks in un-natural colours and forms.

Ascertaining the main characteristic features of this significant school of Iranian painting, we find here that the drawing is bold with a subdued palette of technically inferior pigments to those of Herat, as seen to perfection in the Bodleian *Shah Nāmah* (1420-30). Lapsing with the Turkoman invasions under Shah Isma'il of the Safavid dynasty, the style became simpler and more primitive, employing stronger colours, with the action depicted in the lower area of the painted illustration. At best Safavid-Shiraz produced work which matched with that of Tabriz, but towards the end of the 16th century the painting became 'repetitive' and merely 'decorative'. Overall, Shiraz School has its own uniqueness and its contribution to the Iranian art-heritage is highly admirable and significant. This school, rightly speaking, is an asset of Persian art-world.[13]

(B) THE HERAT SCHOOL OF IRANIAN PAINTING :

The Herat School is one of the significant schools of Iranian painting. Being one of the main centres of Persian painting, Herat left its remarkable effects on the other schools which developed in the later centuries. In Iran during the 15th century the miniature painting achieved high status here at Herat. The impact of the 14th century is also evident here : "The influence of the 14th century, is much in evidence and at Herat under Baysunghur's patronage the art of the miniature reached new heights with the moulding of the best influence of the 14th century in to one style of delicate and aesthetic beauty".[14]

MAIN THEMES AND ARTIST OF HERAT SCHOOL :

The school of Herat especially from 1452 to 1510 flourished under the patronage of Sultan Baysunghur and his successor Sultan Husayn Bayqara. The school was not a new one because its roots were alive in the previous centuries too. It had got its prime position during the 15th century when some of the most famous literary works of Persian creative writer-poets became the central theme for Herat miniature paintings. Literary works such as *Shah Nāmah* of Firdawsi, *Būstān* of Sa'adī; the *Khamsa* of Amir Khusrau of Delhi ("It is certainly a Herati manuscript and shows the direction in which the school there was moving by its disinterest in architectural perspective, compared with the placing of the figures in relations which are both psychological and significans in the whole composition")[15] and few miniatures of the *Gulistān* of Sa'adī; *Khamsa* of Mīr 'Alī Shir Nawai; *Shah Nāmah* of Muhammad Juki; *Zafar Nāmah* (a biography of Timur); *Dīwān-i-Jāmī*, etc. were also executed at the Herat school.[16]

In the field of painting, particularly the miniature painting, the school of Herat proceeded without any break and the artists, like the first Master Artist Mansur's son—Shah Muzaffar, Master Mirak, the famous experienced artist called the Great Bihzad and his pupils, under the patronage of Sultan Husayn, took initiative to bring name and fame to this school :

> ...the school of Herat proceeded without a break, the first master under Sultan Husayn being the son of the court artist of Abu Sa'id, Mansur. This painter, Shah Muzaffar, who was highly praised for his skill, died at the age of twenty-four, and no work by him is known today. Still better known was Master Mirak the painter, a Sayyid or descendant of the Prophet, who was also a monumental calligrapher and an illuminator, before becoming a miniature painter, he became chief of the library of Sultan Husayn and just survived his master's fall, dying soon after the seizure of Herat by the Uzbek, Shaibani Khan, in 1507. But his greatest claim to our attention is that he brought up the future master Bihzad, who had been left an orphan in childhood. he was presumably active from the beginning of the reign.[17]

(a) Bihzad and Herat Renaissance :

Many Persian artists and aestheticians also consider Herat School as the outcome of the unceasing devotion of Bihzad who made Heart a famous school of miniature painting in the Iranian history of aesthetics. In the following lines we shall try to highlight some most important features of Herat school with special reference to its Great Master, Bihzad.

It is an accepted fact that the Herat school of Iranian painting is commonly known through the Master Artist–Bihzad. He devotedly worked for this School under the patronage of sultan Husayin till the seizur of Herat by the Uzbek (Shaibani Khan) in 1507 :

> Bihzad, one of the greatest masters of Persian painting, worked for Sultan Husain in Herat until it was taken by Shah Isma'il, the first of the Safavids. He then moved to Tabriz where he was made director of the Royal Liberary. He may have actually left Herat for Bukhara in 1507, after the conquest by the Uzbegs.[18]

Bihzad was a creative as well as an innovative artist who, with the help of his creative potential and aesthetic sensibility, made a remarkable contribution to the Persian miniature painting, especially to Herat during the latter period of the 15th century. Though we find changes in the art of painting since the second half of the 14th century, yet till the end of the 15th century or even in the latter times, the style and techniques of Bihzad remained popular and indispensable to the Persian painting :

> From late in the 14th century the intrinsic hedonism of the Persians becomes more and more evident through the increased interest in surface decoration at the expence of vitality, and greater elegence and refinement in place of anything actually reminiscent of realism. The most famous name in Persian painting is Bihzad who, at the end of the 15th century, rose above the prevailing interest in mere decoration and, using a line of the utmost delicacy, imbued his characters with the appearance of sustained motion. He was followed, towards the mid-16th, by a group of men who produced the greatest copy of the Poems of Nizami.[19]

As mentioned before, the Herat School of Iranian painting is famous for its traditional Persian **themes** like *Khamsa* of Nizāmī or *Bustan* of Sa'adī. Though the subjects were not original, yet Bihzad, with his techniques, colour schemes and detailed treatment of figures and the natural objects made them masterpieces of Persian painting-world. Bihzad's able pupil, Qasim 'Alī followed him and produced important miniature paintings for Herat school :

> Bihzad was a master of naturalism and expressionism and the figures in his paintings are full of emotion. They are powerful and dramatic. His subjects however were not that original, being drawn from traditional Persian themes like Nizamis Khamsa, but his interpretation was. His paintings are masterpeice of colour and pattern which in no way overwhelms the detailed treatment of the figures. Another artist of Herat who worked in similar style was Qasim 'Alī.[20]

Basil Gray also writes about the Master-artist Bihzad pointing out his creative genius in the field in the following words :

> Bihzad shows his genius for characterization in the way that he has invented here so many poses and groupings that were to become the stoke-in-trade of the Persian school during almost a hundred years. In the construction scene most of the figures form pairs in reciprocal action, thus producing a dynamic pattern of movement which is all contained within the margins and thus built up into a complex of intense energy.[21]

(b) Bihzad and Other Artists :

The 15th century is famous for highlighting the creative potential and aesthetic sensibility of Bihzad and Herat renaissance. During this century, besides Bihzad, other two names 'Alī Sher and Jāmī deserve special mention here. These **three** great artists of Herat renaissance inherited new symbols, spiritual depth, literary taste, and they kept themselves free from the prisons of traditional imagery. Their approach to aesthetics seems mystic in character as they illustrated the works of great Sufi-poets like 'Aṭṭar, Rūmī and Nizāmī:

> All the three visionaries found themselves in the being-in-situation, which Islam had bequeathed to the desert peoples through the parables of the Quran. And they looked for the hidden meaning behind man and woman and flower and bird and fish and dragon and flowing water. But while most people around them were deaf and dumb, their hearts mirrored the glimpses of reality in certain symbols, which could arrest the timeless fire.
>
> The sense of the different layers of reality, the growth of awareness from matter, from the less transitory to the ultimate, had already been bequeathed by Sufi poets like Attar. Rumi and Nizami, in the most subtle allusions.[22]

Bihzad had produced such miniatures as represent the spiritual wholeness. He had an intense awareness of the *mandala*. In this connection M. Ajmal writes in his article, "Paining":

> Mandala represents spiritual wholeness. It seems that Behzad was painting his powerful pictures not to produce decorative effects but to answer a spiritual need. it was a response to his spiritual longing, a colourful realm discovered by his spiritual quest, as answer to the prayers of his soul. When one looks at "The Dancing Derishes," one finds that compared with it the most renowned mandala painting by the mystics of other creeds pale into insignificance. The spell that Behzad's paintings cast on the beholder can radiate only from a whole soul. It is not the work of a mere decorator.[23]

So far as the subject-matter or theme of the Herat miniature paintings is concerned it is, as mentioned before, essentially based on the literary works of most important Persian Suif-poets and creative writers. In every miniature, Bihzad tried to search for external-internal meaning and secrets of Reality in different ways. Bihzad had beautifully portrayed Man-God-Universe relationship in his works :

> In the themes chosen for miniatures, from the *Bostan* of Sa'adi (Cairo National Library) as well as Nizami's *Khamsa* and the *Khamsa* of Amir Khusrau, are subjects like *Two Mosques, the incident of Sultān Dārā and the herdsman, Yūsuf and Zuleikha, Laila and Majnu at School, Majnu Watching the battle of the tribes* and the *Hammam scene, Dancing Dervishes, Shirin Receiving Khusrau at her Palace in Armenia, Behram Gaur killing a Dragon.*
>
> In every one of these pictures Bihzad searches for a double meaning.
>
> Furthermore, not only does he perfect all the element of miniature painting before him, but introduces a drama in each painting. From the 14th century onwards there had been an emphasis on 'pretty' pictures. The finest fine brushwork had been achieved with meticulous care for detail in the assemblage of many coloured universes, reproducing, at its loveliest, in the flowers and grasses and shrubs and cypresses and flowing streams and twittering birds, background in which were seated lovely queens and magnificent heroes, drinking and talking. And there had been achieved heroic scenes, symbolically indicating action by adjusting figures within the rectangular framwork.[24]

Thus we see that Bihzad's choice of the theme for his miniature in every manscript indicates his search for double [wordly and Divinly] meaning in the legend he decides to be illustrated. So, it becomes very easy to recognize the Herat paintings executed by Bihzad in a daramatic way. In this regard Ernst Kuhnel writes in his article "History of Miniature Painting and Drawing" that "The Herat school was never content with just a good, workmanlike performance, but artistic individualities constantly emerged, so that it is quite consistent that a master of the importance of Bihzad should have come to fore there." Infact, the characteristic tendencies of the Herat school are especially well exemplified in the *Shah Nāmah* made for Muhammad Jukī, the son of Shah Rukh. In these miniatures, the foces are clear and expressive and the shades of the garments clearly show the preference for deeper, warmer coloures which later become a distinctive feature of identification in the Herat works. It was the creative and aesthetically rich-minded Bihzad who made Herat an important school of Iranian Painting. He is to Herat School as soul is to body. The rank of Bizad in the history of mankind is assured through his recreations of his heart's desires in some of the most perfect pictures painted by man, through which we con see the face of the beloved.[25]

In the **conclusion** we can understand that the Herat School represents the peak of refinement in Persian painting. Sultan Baysunghur assembled at his court some of the leading artists of his day, who produced, in a remarkably short span of time, work of the highest quality. His successor, Sultan Husayn Bayqara, also took great pains in the development of this school. The composition of the paintings of this school observes the traditional formulae: use of diagonal or circular forms, a concentration of detail to the left. We find elongated figures with over-large heads and frail-looking horses dominate the scenes. A Chinese influence is apparent but highly stylised in cloud, flame, rock and tree treatment with the popular mystical symbols like animals and birds or other natural objects etc., in the miniature-art of Herat School.

By the end of the 16th century (A.D.) the accent is on decorative motifs in elaborate compositions such as small rocks. twisted flowering trees, polygonal pavilions with tile-work and railings in the background and ducks on ponds in the foreground frequent the miniatures. This was to be continued in the later Persian schools and its influence seems immense on the Ottoman calligraphic drawings and Mughal painting. These were some important characteristic features of the Herat School of Iranian miniature painting.

(See Plate 15 , 16).

(C) TABRIZ SCHOOL OF IRANIAN PAINTING :

In the history of Persian painting Tabriz schools' contribution has special importance. Though due to political ups and downs this cannot be considered a real centre of Timurid art, yet we find enough evidence to ascertain its uniqueness in its two phases–during the **fourteenth** and the **sixteenth** centuries.

Tabriz school was too famous for its art-activity in the 13th century and the famous miniature paintings of the manuscript *Manafi-al-Hayawan* were executed under the patronage of Ganza Khan–the first Il-Khanid Sultan interested in this field. Subsequently Hulagu took up the manuscript for the calligraphy but few paintings were available :

> Under Gazna Khan, who made Tabriz the capital and ruled from 1295 to 1304 AD., the new faith became the State religion. This Sultan was the first Il-Khanid to patronise the painting of a manuscript, the Manafi-al-Hayawan, now in the Morgan collection in New York.... The calligraphy of the Manafi-al-Hayawan manuscript was done at Muragha, where Hulagu had established his observatory. There are ninety-four miniatures in this manuscript, of which twelve seem to have been executed at the time of the writing, and the rest are by some other hand. The painting juts out often from the rectangle of the Arab pictorial situation, as though bursting out of the conventional space

allotted to it in the text. The animal figures are emphasised, with the foliage used merely as background. extension of calligraphy.[26]

In the 14th century we find here in Tabriz the Mongol style which was distinctively developed under the Il-Khans. As we know, the powerful Mongol chief, Hulagu, a younger brother of Chinghiz Khan, appeared in 1253 (A.D.) and took Baghdad in 1258-1336 (A.D.) which ruled the old Abbasid territories, and more, till 1336 A.D. when the Il-Khanids were set aside by a Jalayr prince.[27] So, in order to highlight the main features of the Tabriz school of Iranian painting it is essential to know the themes and personalities of this school.

MAIN THEMES AND ARTISTS OF TABRIZ SCHOOL :

Tabriz emerged as an important centre for the book-painting. It had imbided in its styles and techniques all the main features of other schools such as Shiraz and Herat and the best example in this connection is the **Rashid al-**Din's copies of the late 14th century :

> ... the new orientation given to the arts and especially to book painting in the very active ateliers of Shiraz and Herat could not fail to impress the Tabriz masters, though the innovations that came to their attention seem merely to have inspired superficial compromises, as if they were trying to maintain as long as possible the traditional style, represented by the Rashid al-din copies of the late fourteenth century.[28]

We must note that their is no fixed date of starting or closing any of the Persian schools of painting. Certain manuscripts had been started for illustration in one century and completed in another century or reillustrated again and again under the patronage of different rulers or Sultans.

Some most important manuscripts illustrated in this school include *Jami'al Tawarikh*. (Universal-History) of Rashid al-Din, *Al-Athar al-Baqiyah* (History of Ancient People), *Shah Namah* (Demotte of Firdausi), *Kalila wa Dimna* (Album from the Imperial Palace of Yildiz) etc. all were executed in the 14th century under the patronage of different Persian kings.[29] **(See Plate 11,17**

There are elements of Chinese art in the works of Tarbiz school especially in the illustrations of *Jami'al-Tawarikh* of Rashid al-Din :

> The most conspicuous of all the Chinese borrowings in the miniatures of this period are the trees and mountains. These can hardly have been derived from any source but actual paintings, access to which is likely to have been derived from any source but actual paintings, access to which is likely to have been derived from any source but actual paintings, access to which is likely to have been limited to court circles. We know that there were Chinese scholars at the capital Tabriz, and that the Wazir, Rashid al-Din, had Chinese helpers in compiling his universal history. It is in the Tabriz manuscripts that the Chinese Landscape occur in their purest from; that is, in the Morgan Bestiary and the two surviving portions of the Jami'al-Tawarikh, dating from the lifetime of this author, Rashid al-Din.[30]

The Chinese models have provided inspiration only for details and for the use of grey and brown. The final result was a synthesis of all arts. Besides *Jami'al-Tawarikh*. we find the Chinese influence in the *al-Athar al-Baqiyah* (History of Ancient People) of al-Biruni. In this connection we would like to mention only one illustration of this manuscript : *'Destruction of the Temple of Jerusalem* (executed in Tabriz in 1307-8 A.D.). In the Universal History (*Jami'al-Tawarikh*) two important illustrations *'The Sacred Tree of Buddha'*

(See Plate 11) and '*Abrāham Receiving the Three Strangers and Sarah in the Tent*' are the miniatures in which we clearly find the Chinese motif :

> Possibly these represent the Chinese heavy brushstroke made with the side of the brush, but they might be referred more naturally to the imitation of embroidery or tapestry weaving. The shading within these contours is much richer in the other manuscripts of the group, especially the Jami-al-Tawarikh and the History of Ancient Peoples by al-Biruni, also in the liberary of Edinburgh University (Arab 161). We find the same Jagged contours but enriched by strong colour, in earthy tints, chocolate brown, stateblue, and brown ochre, often strongest near the summits and enclosing curious bubble like reserves which are perhaps intended to represent stones; or filled with internal contour systems which may indeed be used to convey the same information as the contour in a modern map. If so, this would be a useful indication of the fundamentally symbolic character even of this most naturalistic sort of Persian book-painting. So that although in the Jami-al-Tawarikh the colouring is so much more subdued and limited, the basic concept is usually, nearer to the Persian conceptual picture.[31]

Underlining the general style of Tabriz tradition, A.U. Pope writes with special reference to one of the *Shah Nāmah's* miniatures (especially the painting which shows Timur seated before a tent in the midst of a festive outdoor gathering). It is believed that this miniature, with its special details, belonged to the 15th century :

> An interesting miniature from a *Shah-Nāmah* in the possession of Kevorkian, New York, belongs probably to this class of illustrations of the Turkoman period. The painting, which covers two pages and served originally as a frontispiece, shows Timur seated before a tent in the midst of a festive outdoor gathering, on a carpet which bears in the border a laudatory inscription and the date 1389 (791H.). In the grouping, positions, and costumes of the courtiers, the servants bringing refreshments, the musicians, and all the other personages, the picture accords completely in

> general style with the Tabriz tradition; but the scene evidently was not recorded by an eye witness, for, save for Timur himself, none of the figures has the character of a portrait. The marginal arabesque decoration is unmistakably later, as are several details of the setting, which leads us to believe that the miniature must be classed as a work of the fifteenth century, in spite of the earlier date.[32]

In Tabriz school of Iranian painting some other important miniature paintings of *Shah Nāmah* of Firdawsī include particularly '*Battle of Iskandar with the Dragon*'; '*The Indian Army fleeing before the Iron Warriors of Iskandar*'; '*The Bier of the Great Iskandar*' —————————— [all executed during 1330-1336] deserve special consideration in order to ascertain the technique, style and tradition of this school. In brief "the *Shah Namah* pictures sum up and transcend all that can be found of drama and decorative richness in the earlier Tabriz book. The colouring of the al-Biruni is combined with the movements of the *Jami' al-Tawarikh*, while the role of landscape has increased, and it is brought into closer relation with the figures".[33]

Now we shall briefly discuss the **second** phase of Tabriz school which started in the 16th century (A.D.) and patronized by the Safavid rulers. This school is also known as 'the Safavi School' under Shah-Tahmasp.

During the Safavid period Tabriz school effectively flourished and contributed a lot in the field of miniature painting of Iran. The base of the work as usual, was manuscripts of the important personalities. Famous Master painters like Bihzad, Mir Sayyid 'Alī, Shaikh Zada, Khwaja 'Abd al-Aziz, Āqā Mirak, Sultan Muḥammad, Shah Muḥammad, Mir Naqqash, Shaikh Muḥammad.

Muzaffar 'Alī, Mirza 'Alí and 'Abd al-Samad (who was also trained in Tabriz and went to India with the Mughals) worked with devotion and sincerity here at Tabriz and brought name and fame to this school. Other important painters in Tabriz school include Kamal, Shah Quli, Vali Jan (who later on went to Istanbul), Inayat Allah, Ustad Muhammadi, etc. etc. were equally the artists of eminence who made Tabriz a centre and spring of all creative artistic activity.[34]

Due to the uncertain political situation, Tabriz could not get its true prime status. However, when the Safavids captured Herat, all the court painters moved to the Safavid Court at Tabriz--a centre where the classical style was still continued. The Safavid Kings brought some changes in the motif of the miniature painting. The great Master Artist, Bihzad moved from Herat to Tabriz and he was made director of the Royal library :

> There is a decree of Shah Ismail in Khwandamir's compilation *Naam ye-Naami* about the appointement of Bihzad by Shah Ismail as Director of the Imperial Library and from the story of Ali, the art historian, that this king evinced great anxiety about the safety of Bihzad during the was against Sultan Salim I, in 1514 A.D.
>
> As Royal Librarian of Shah Ismail, Bihzad was put in charge of all other librarians, calligraphers, painters, guilders, marginal draftsmen, gold mixers, gold beaters and lapis lazuli washers.
>
> Obviously, then, Bihzad had moved to Tabriz under Shah Ismail, and continued to work under this king's successor, Shah Tahmasp. This fact is confirmed by Kazi Ahmad whosays that Bihzad contributed miniatures to the copy of the *Khamsa* of Nizami, prepared by the calligrapher Shah Muhammad.
>
> Ustad Bihzad seems to have received many honours from Shah Tahmasp, who was a keen patron of the arts, and the master

continued to work with Aga Mirak and Sultan Muhammad in the library.[35]

Thus, under the patronage of the Safavids rulers, especially Shah Tahmasp, a new but important style had evolved at Tabriz and the artists of the great calibre produced paintings of outstanding subtlety and grace:

> During the early part of the 16th century there was considerable movement of artists from one court to another, due to the unsettled political situation. After the Safavid Court at Tabriz, where the classical style continued, greatly influenced by Baghdad. Mir Syeed Ali of Tabriz, a painter of great talent, was to have a profound effect on the formation of the Moghul School of paintings, when he founded the court atelier of the Moghul Emperor Akbar. This was after the Safavid ruler, Shah Thamasp had withdrawn his patronage of painting.
>
> Persian painting had been greatly dependent on Royal patronage, and this withdrawal of Royal assent was nothing short of a catastrophe. Many of the best painter left the court, some like Mir 'Ali, went to the Moghul court in India. Others stayed finding alternative patronage in Persia. Paintings patronized the court were extremely expensive to produce, so much so the ex-royal artists had to modify their paintings to suit the pocket of their less wealthy patrons.
>
> The result was a change from sumptuously illustrated manuscripts to simpler miniature paintings and drawings. Changes also occurred in the paintings themselves. The occasional practice of extending the subject beyond its borders now became the norm. Elements of landscapes were modified and figures became less realistic until by the end of the 16th century, the human figure had taken on an entirely different dimension. Both line and tinted drawings were extremely popular.[36]

No doubt Tabriz school got its full glory and fame under the patronage of Shah Tahmasp. However, in the end of his tenure, a new, but radiant style had come into being at this great centre of Iranian art and various great Master artists like Mirak and Ustad 'Alī produced marvellous paintings using bright colours and depicting human and non-human figures :

> Before Shah Tahmasp withdrew his patronage, a new and brilliant style had evolved at Tabriz, under a number of great artists including Mirak, Sultan Muhammad and Ustad Ali. Their eye for harmonious colour produced painting of outstanding subtlety and delicacy. Deep blues, gold and a Kaleidoscope of colourful flowers feast the eye. Animals, birds and humans are all animated with superb skill.[37]

The main themes during this period of the 16th century of Tabriz school were almost the same as executed or undertaken by the Herat artists. In most of the Persian schools of painting the same themes like book illustration or book-painting recur time and again with certain minor changes. In some schools we do not find even the change in style and technique. In this connection we refer to Bihzad's paintings of Herat and Tabriz where we do not find any major change though his pupils developed new styles in new environment :

> When in 1522 (928 H.) Shah Isma'il made Bihzad Director of his Library and of the studio for producing books, he had already had a decade of productive work in Tabriz. We know nothing about his predecessor, but undoubtedly Bihzad from the very beginning dominated the new development of miniature painting there. He did not change his style in any essential respects, so that a distinction can scarcely be made between his Herat and his Tabriz periods. He remained fundamentally a Khurasani, and when he moved to Tabriz his development had long since come to a standstill.
>
> The pupils that Bihzad took with him from Herat, on the contrary, developed to such an extent in their new environment that they must be considered wholly of the school of Tabriz.[38]

CONCLUSION :

To sum up the discussion on the Tabriz School it has been noticed that in the history of Persian painting, the contribution of Tabriz deserves special appreciation. Tabriz, as we know, being the capital of Safavid Persia under Shah Isma'il was undoubtedly a flourishing cultural centre and its school of painting was famous and much admired. The great Master artists of Tabriz School were Mīr Sayyīd 'Alī, Sultan Muḥammad and Mirak. It was strongly dependent on the Herat School many of whose artists had moved from there to the new capital. Thus, the style continued to use a number of the earlier conventions, range of pallette and brush-strokes, but with certain differences. Later the individuality of the great master Bihzads, human figures is lost with the miniature increasing in size. In Iranian art-tradition Tabriz excelled in genere painting. Everyday-scenes are depicted with a keen observation of detail and the figures are seen as the **realistic** portraits rather than stylised types. The artists of the school preferred and adopted the realistic attitude in their creative products. (See Plate **11,17**).

(D) QAZVIN SCHOOL OF IRANIAN PAINTING :

The Persian miniature painting is in scale the most delicate and aesthetically rich art of Iranians. The fine art form is the most brilliant painting ever executed by man. In the creation of this important art form the Persian Schools of miniature painting played a pivotal role. Among the prominent schools of Iranian painting, some of which we have discussed earlier, the Qazvin is also important in various respects. We must keep it in our mind that almost all the schools of Iranian art are inter-linked and there is no fixed date of starting or ending of any school.

The approximate date of the Qazvin School has been mentioned as the mid of the 16th century till the end of 17th century A.D.[39] This Persian school of painting named after the town of Qazvin, which became the capital city as well as the prominent art centre under the Safavid Shah Tahmasp (1526-76). Like other schools (such as Shiraz and Tabriz) of the Safavid Shahs this school has also got the equal importance in creating and contributing significantly to Islamic art.

The Qazvin's existence as a separate school has been an acknowledged fact. Additionally, it has a more dignified form than the work of the earlier Tabriz school. The Safavid Kings were very found of art, literature and culture and therefore, through establishing schools and encouraging the talented artists they fulfilled their inner aesthetic urge.

MAIN THEME AND ARTISTS OF QAZVIN SCHOOL :

The main theme of the Qazvin school of Persian miniature painting has mainly been Jami's manuscripts (poems) *Haft Awrang* and *Yūsuf and Zulaikha*. But the first manuscript (*Haft Awrang*) become the chief subject-matter for the school. The miniature - work seems to have been a combination of the Tabriz and Qazvin styles though it is believed that

Shah Tahmasp lost interest in painting in his later years yet the art-tradition of the Safavids was enthus - iastically carried out by his nephew, prince Ibrahim Mirza.

The above text was executed few years ago but some modifications were made here at Qazvin art-centre:

> Persia begin truly unified under the Safavids, the metropolitan court style naturally moved with the capital of the country. This was at first Tabriz, but that city was soon found to be too vulnerable to Turkish attacks, and in 1548 the court moved to Qazvin. In his later years Shah Tahmasp lost interest in painting and became a religious bigot, but the tradition of enlightened princely patronage was maintained by his nephew Prince Ibrahim Mirza, who held his court at Mashhad. A magnificent manuscript of Jami's poems, the *Half Aurang* or Seven Thrones, ... is the best surviving monument to the prince's taste and munificence. The text dates from between 1556 and 1565 and the miniatures admirably illustrate the transition between the Tabriz style of Tahmasp's early years and mature style of Qazvin. They are, as usual in manuscripts of the first quality, the work of several hands, and while some are almost indistinguishable stylistically from work done for Tahmasp twenty years earlier, others, presumably painted by younger and more progressive artists, show a number of modifications in figure drawing and composition.[40]

The prominent characteristic features of this schools' miniature paintings seem that the line of the bodies are sinuour and graceful and long necks and round faces appear prominently. The drawing is firm and simple. Different stages of human life as well as the dresses have been represented skilfully. In all the miniatures of the Qazvin school the naturalistic elements got prominence:

> The sinuous lines of the slim, youthful figures are still further emphasized, and the enclosing frame of the miniature, over which parts of the composition had been allowed to spill from early Timurid times, is now sometimes entirely disregarded. Whilst the faces of youths and maidens are rounder and smoother than ever, those of middle-aged and elderly characters are often naturalistic to the point of caricature. The baton turban, distinguishing badge of the Safavid house in its early years, was disappearing, being replaced by a neat round turban of modest dimensions.[41]

Prince Ibrahim Mirza was the son of Barham Mirza, who upto great extent patronized the school while his uncle withdrew his patronage. Maulana Malik, a renowned Master Calligrapher, was the personal instructor of the Prince. For sometimes he was nominated as the governor of Meshhed and Malik went with him. But after some years he was recalled by the Shah to Qazvin where he was required to write the inscription on the new government buildings then under construction. This was not later than 1561, but he had meanwhile set going. One of the most surviving achievements of the period was the manuscript of the *Haft Awrang* of Jāmi. Various artists of the Qazvin school executed twenty-eight miniatures from this manuscript in nine years' time:

> ... the manuscript of the *Haft Aurang* of Jami, now in the Freer Gallery in Washington. With its twenty-eight miniatures this took nine years to complete, and the copying was completed by his successor in-charge of the library, Muhibb Ali, his father Rustam Ali (who had previously worked for the prince's father, Bahram Mirza), Ayshi of Herat and Shah Mahmud, the most famous of them all. These scribes are all mentioned with high praise by Qadi Ahmad, who was brought up in Meshhed where his father

> was a wazir for ten years, apparently just at the time of the preparation of this sumptuous manuscript. Consequently the account which he gives of the leading painters who were then working in the prince's library is likely to be accurate and inclusive. It is therefore to these hands that its twenty - eight miniatures must be attributed: Shaykh Muhammad, ʿAlī Asghar, and ʿAbdullah.[42]

Both Jāmī's *Yūsuf and Zulaikha* and *Haft Awrang* are illustrated with originality by numerous painters. Several figures appear so often that they are easily recognized. The best examples of the Qazvin school for our present purpose are: *Two lovers landing on the Island of Terrestial Bliss* (from *Haft Awrang* of Jāmī) *Yūsuf on the Market-place* (from *Yūsuf and Zuliaikha* of Jāmī).(See Plate 12 , 14).

The *Haf Awrang* manuscript was finished in 1565 and since Ibrahim survived for another twelve years there must have been much else produced for him which it is not now easy to identify. Another Jami's manuscript copied by Shah Mehmud of Meshhed containing only the *Yūsuf and Zulaikha* on large paper with twelve full page miniatures shows a similar interest in complicated street scenes with many figures. This manuscript, as it is said, is attributed to Meshhed: "This is most simply explained if the manuscript is attributed to Meshhed, where the scribe is stated to have remained for twenty years, following the change of heart of his old patron shah Tahmasp, until his death there in 1564-1565. These miniatures may have been finished during the next five years or so by Ibrāhīm's Staff."[43]

Some prominent master artists of the Qazvin school of Iranian miniature painting include Sadiqi Beg. Mirak, Mir Muṣawwir, Mir Sayyid 'Alī, Shaikh Muḥammad Shirazi. Muḥammadī, Muzuffar 'Alī, Shah, Muḥammad, 'Alī Asghar, 'Abdullah. Shaykh Muḥammad etc. Their eye, for harmonious colours, produced painting of outstanding subtlety and delicacy. In their works we find deep blues, gold and a Kaleidoscope of colourful flowers feast the sight. In their miniature paintings we see that animals, birds and human being and other natural objects are shown with superb skill. We also find in those paintings a little influence of Chinese motif of miniature painting especially 'cloud forms' and 'dresses'. Sadiqi Beg was the meritorious artist of all of them and he was rightly projected as an exponent of the mature Qazvini style. Thus the Qazvin School has its own importance and uniqueness in the history of Iranian miniature painting.

E. ISFAHAN SCHOOL OF IRANIAN PAINTING

Iran has long been famous for its different art-forms such as architecture, calligraphy*, pottery, painting, poetry. book-illustration and so on. Persia developed several distinctive styles and techniques in the field of her art-activity and hence, various schools emerged on the soil of *Fars* (Iran). The Isfahan School is one of them which was established during the end of the 16th century (A.D.) under the Safavid Sultān Shah, 'Abbās (I) (1587-1629).

* *(See Plate 19).*

As we know, the Safavid Kings emerged at the beginning of the 16th century and rescued Iran form political chaos and fragmentation. Indeed in many ways the Safavid dynasty marks the beginnings of Modern Iranian history for they secured the North-Eastern frontier and no longer was Iran troubled by massive invasions from Central Asia and beyond. The Safavid Sultans' love for aesthetics made them to establish various schools of art such as Tabriz and Isfahan.

In the last quarter of the 16th century Isfahan became the centre of Iranian art-tradition. "By the end of the 16th century Isfahan had become Persia's capital and its present magnificence reflects the central role which it then played in the development of so many facets of Iranian art".[44]

Isfahan was not only the prime centre of Iranian art-activity but a fine school of Muslim intellectual activity as well. Various important philosophers, Sufis and other founders of some movements emerged form here. Without Isfahan's significant contribution to *Ḥikmat* (Philosophy) and *Fun* (Art) Muslim intellectual history seems incomplete :

> This form of wisdom or *Ḥikmat*, some features of which we have sought to out line here; did not die with the termination of the Safawid dynasty. In the thirteenth/eighteenth century Sufism was revived in Persia by Ma'sūm 'Alī Shah and Shah Tahir Dakani, two Ni'matullahi masters sent by Rida' 'Ali Shah from Deccan to Persia. It was persecuted for a period but began to expand with the establishment of the Qajars. Likewise, the school of *Ḥikmat* continued through the students of Mulla Sadra and others from one generation to another until it produced *Shaikk* Ahmad

> Ahsa'i, the founder of the Shaikhi movement, Haji Mulla Hadi Sabizwari, and several other outstanding figures in the Qajar period, the light of whose teachings has not yet disappeared from the horizon of Persia. One can hardly understand the intellectual life of Islam in its totality without taking into account this last major period of Muslim intellectual activity, lasting from the Safawid period to the present,...[45]

In the field of miniature painting the Isfahan school of Iranian art remained the main centre of Eastern Islamic Culture about two hundred years. The Qazvin and Herat styles were prevalent in Isfahan school. Riza Abbasi's works and other manuscripts, such a *Gulistān* and so on, became the model for the subsequent-century painting.

> Under the Safawid Sultan Shah Abbas I (1587-1629) the Persian Capital was moved to Isfahan (1598) where for nearly two hundered years it became the centre of eastern Islamic Culture. Sadiki Beg became head of the court scriptorium bringing the Qazvin drawing style to Isfahan. His successor as leading artist there was Riza Abbasi whose work became the model for all subsequent 17th Century painting. At the beginning of the century there was a revival in Isfahan of the Herat style, perhaps to be explained by the presence in Shah Abbas's library of such manuscripts as the *Gulistān Shah nāma* (1430). Some of these Neo-Timurid manuscripts were as brilliant in technique as the original.[46]

MAIN THEMES OF ISFAHAN SCHOOL

Like other schools of Persian painting the Isfahan has same subject matter —— literary, ethical, religious and classical manuscripts. Under the patronage of Shah Abbās(I) Isfahan school illustrated manuscripts such as

Gulistān Sahanāmah, and chiefly the works of a leading artist Riza Abbasi. Besides the development in other art-forms, some paintings of the school do represent the background of the Shah's own life :

> The monarchy of Shah Abbas I was an efficient bureaucracy, reflecting in all its departments the aims and taste of the Shah. His love of splendour and interest in architecture are reflected in the central area of the Median at Isfahan, surrounded by the tile-covered buildings of the mosques and the gates of the bazaars, and dominated by the tall palace of the 'Ali Qapu; form which he was accustomed to look down on the busy city set in ample gardens. Only the painted decoration of this building seems inadequate to the setting. There was no real tradition to the setting. There was no real tradition of wall-painting in Safavi Persia; but it might have been expected that the royal taste which directed the sumptuous brocade-weaving and tile-designing not to speak of the famous carpet-weaving in the royal factories might have required something more nobles from his painters to decorate the private apartments of his palace. But these paintings of young pages and courtiers do represent the background to the Shah's own life, ...
>
> Such were the commissions given to the royal painters; and it is therefore not surprising that the leading painter of this age should have been Riza Abbasi, whose active career seems to have extended from 1610 to 1640.[47]

The illustrated manuscript of the *Shah Nāmh* was prepared for Shah Abbas(I) in 1614. In this connection we shall refer to one miniature namely *Kay Khusrau offering the Crown to Luhrarp* (1614) form the *Shahh Nāmah* of Shah Abbas(I).

It is said that thirty nine miniatures are pastiches of the famous Baysunghur *Shah Nāmah* in the *Gulistān* Palace in Tehran and a careful comparison shows that twenty two of the compositions are closely repeated with occasional simplification by omission of one or two figures, and more regularly by the addition of more foreground rocks and more background trees. In simple words we can say that the same subject-matter has been represented in Isfahan school with certain minor changes.[48]

The Isfahan School is also known as Riza-i-Abbasi's school. The contribution of this great artist deserve special recognition. Under the able guidance of Shah Abbas(I), Riza Abbasi produced outstanding paintings :

> When, however, Shah 'Abbas ((1587-1628) (995-1037 H.)) changed his residence to Isfahan and stimulated all the arts to one last great achievement by his prodigal orders, painting also entered into a new phase. Isfahan became the direct heir of Tabriz, yet it is not difficult to define the boudary that marks at once the juxtaposition and the differentiation between the two schools. The outstanding personality in Isfahan was Riza 'Abbasi, and we have a great many authentic signed and dated worked by him.[49]

The first painter who can virtually be separated out from the mass of "Riza" material (as the very 'surname' beared confusion in Isfahan School) can quite possibly be known as Aqa Riza Murid or '*the pupil*' as he himself preferred and applied this designation. Ernst Kuhnel writes that he had but little contact with the Isfahan school and seems to have carried on his chief art-activity at the Mughal court in India.[50]

The second personality whose works became the theme in the field of miniature painting of the Isfahan School is clearly defined and known as Raza Abbasi. The list of his main works (where his indubitable signatures are all in the same form) even in the first-half of the 16th century, are as under. According to A.U. Pope this list comprises absolutely dependable documents from which further attribution can be made :

Year	Name of miniature painting and its placement
1618	(1028 H.) ***Majnūn in the Desert***, copied from a composition of the school of Bihzad; now in the *Gulistān Museum*, formerly in the possession of *H. Kevorkian*.
1622	(1031 H.) ***Darvish Resting*** : *Bibliotheque Nationale*.
1624	(1034 H.) ***Standing Cubearer with a fur cap*** ; formerly *Homberg Collection*.
1626	(1035 H.) ***Bird on the Stump of a Tree***, in the background a shurb, persumably after Bihzad, with an inscription added in 1630 I1040 H.) ; present ownership unknown.
1626	(1035 H.) ***Majnūn Scene*** ; formerly in the possession of *Charles Vignier*.
1627	(1037 H.) ***Woman with a Mirror leaning on a Cushion covered witha figural fibric*** ; owner unknown ; formerly in *Tehran*.
1628	(1037 H.) ***Young man wearing a European hat, standing*** ;

Khanenko Collection Kiev.

1628 (1037 H.) ***Young man in European costume, standing***; collection of Mr. A. Morrison. (A variant of this picture, said to represent Sir Anthony or Sir Robert Sherley, belonging to *Miss H. Schlesinger*, is clearly by an imitator.)

1630 (1039 H.) ***Pair of lovers*** ; collection of *Professor Sarre.*

1631 (1041 H.) ***Portrait of the Darvish 'Abd al-Muṭallib***; *Library of the Academy, Leningrad.*

1631 (1041 H.) ***Drawing of a Darvish***, made for the '**Sultan of the Poor**', '*Abd al-Malik of Astarabad*; *Boston Museum* of Fine Arts.

1632 (1041 H.) ***Shepherd with Sheep and Goats***; collection of *Miss H Sutherland.*

Again, the drawing-style is identical with a coloured miniature in the Library of the Academy, Leningrad, which shows the same subject even more effectively treated and certainly cannot be later in date. The inscription had been cut off but the signature is still distinct. Some more examples are as under:

1632 (1041 H.) ***Pair of Lovers*** ; collection M.J.J. Marquet de Vasselot.

1632 (1041 H.) ***Man with Snakes*** ; formerly *possession of Demotte*, Paris.

1633 (1033 H.) ***Shah Safi and the physician Muḥammad Shamsa,*** *with the Shah's horse and two pager* ; *State Library*, Leningrad.

1634 (1034 H.) ***Portuguese drinking***, with a Dog ; *Metropolitan Museum of Art.*

1634 (1044 H.) ***Figure drawn for the son of the painter, Muhammad Shafi*** ; formerly in the *possession of Demotte*, Paris.[51]

There are also other works which cannot be accepted as authentic until they have been further studies and verified that whether or not they should be attributed to Riza-i-Abbasi as the Chief Master artist of Isfahan. Actually there are different signatures bearing the same name '*Riza*' which brought confusion as to who was the real painter. Besides '*Riza-e Ábbāsī*, an other name, as mentioned before, is that of *Āqa Riza-i-Murīd* who had signed variously as '*Áqa Riza*', '*Muḥammad Riza*', '*Äqa Muḥammad Riza*', '*Murid*' or *Murīd-i-Padishāh* and so on.[52] But it is a fact that most of the works of Isfahan School belonged to the Master painter Riza-i-Ábbāsī only. Though there are *some* paintings which attributed to him while, on the other, "the inscription *Áqā Riza* is not in his writings and must be a letter addition"[53]

MAIN ARTISTS AND THEIR CONTRIBUTION :

In the development of the Isfahan School of Iranian painting the contribution of Riza Ábbāsī is immense and unique. He was a fine painter and draughtsman having his own colour-scheme and techniques. He gave a new life to Persian art-tradition. Shah Ábbas(I) admired him much for his different styles in different art-forms such as calligraphy, miniature painting, textile art, abstract designs in the arts of illumination and carpet-making etc. It is said that his son Shafi was also a brilliant designer in the field of textile. When we see the works of Riza Abbasi and his son Shafi, we find that they had incorporated the tendency of '*realism*' in their creative products. Basil Gray describes about Riza 'Abbāsī and his son Shafi in the following words :

> That he was a brilliant draughtsman may be seen from the famous sarre sketchbook now in the Freer Gallery, Washington. And this fluent penmanship with thickened accent and spluttered termination underlies all his genuine work, much of which is fully coloured with flat enamelled pigment which takes a craquelure. These may befinished with gold brocade designs on dresses. What distinguishes him from his followers and imitators is his interest in pure design; the ample folds of a long scarf or a dervish's clock, the ends of a page's sash are emphasized to a degree which gives them an abstract beauty, which is picked up in the gold painting of the background, in which gives them an abstract beauty, which is picked up in the gold painting of the background, in which the silhouettes of wine-bottles or fruit are incorporated into the sprays of chenar foliage and the wisps of cloud to form an all-over pattern of expressive brushwork. The design is on the point of dissolving into free abstraction which might have led Persia to an art well suited to her long tradition of calligraphy and abstract design in the arts of illumination and carpet-marking. That there was a connexion between the work of Shah Abbas' painters and his textile factories is in any case very probable, and we shall see that Shafi the son Riza was definitely a designer for textiles. Unfortunately the tendency to **realism**. which was competing with this abstract designing, gained the upper hand, perhaps mainly under the influence of European art in which the Shah took an interest for its own sake, and which represented the market which he was concerned to capture for the export of brocads.[54]

Other important artist who worked for the development of the Isfahan School include Muḥammad Yūsuf al-Ḥusainī, Mu'īn, Mīr Afzāl Tūnī, Ḥabīb Allāh, Malik Ḥusayn, Shah Qāsim etc. and all worked mainly in the style of their great Master artist—Riza 'Abbāsī :

> To them, however, together with other members of the atelier can be attributed the vast number of brush drawings and miniatures which have been incorrectly ascribed to Riza 'Abbāsī himself. If can not be denied that they often correspond with Riza's work so completely in all details that distinctive indications of another authorship, such as are found in Western art, cannot be descried.[55]

Yet other best representatives of the School in the later generation are Muḥammed Qāsim and Muḥammed 'Alī, who also worked in Riza's general style but were more directly related to Mu'in. The painter Mu'in who in many respects had clearly marked out a way for himself, and thereby these two artist "arrived at a rather superficial but pleasing, purely decorative miniature style which was enlivened by a bright colour scale. These paintings can no longer be confused with the work of Riza's own pupils.[56] Among the above mentioned famous artists we would like to refer here Muḥammad Yūsuf al-Ḥusainī's important miniature painting '*Love Scene*'. He was a contemporary of Riza 'Abbāsī and carried out the traditional Persian figure-drawing method in this works. Regarding the above-mentioned composition of al-Ḥusainī, Basil Gray gives a fine description in the following lines :

> In a brilliant composition now preserved in the Morgan Library he makes of the relations of three figures, two kneeling young men and a standing lady of fashion whose waist one of them is embracing, an exercise in intersecting forms which for once is composed in depth. Her upraised arms coil about the turban which she has removed from her lover's head and is placing on her own, in a dance movement echoed by the streaming clouds and foliage against the deep blue sky. Little is known by this artist but his masterly draughtsmanship is illustrated in the Pozzi and Dawud collections.[57]

In the reign of Shah 'Abbās II (1642-1667) the Isfahan School of Iranian miniature painting innovated various new techniques and styles in the art of painting under his patronage. He tried to review the given trend of Riza Abbasi in the miniature-art of Persia and clearly realized the danger of complete stagnation of Persian art of painting. He suggested the measures of developing the art and with the result the Shah II had sent some selected students, by giving them scholarships, to work with talented Master artists trained in Western workshops. One of these young artists, who got his training in Rome, is Muhammad Zaman in whose work we find the Western influence. In this connection we would prefer to refer here to one of his three miniatures that he added to the Nizami's work made for Shah Tahmasp. In this one important miniature '*Barhám Gur's contest with the Dragon*' is shown. All the three paintings as well as some others from *Shah Nāmah*, he painted in the same year (1675). With his creative activity, colour compositions and new techniques he had contributed a lot to the Isfahan school :

> It seems to have been Shah 'Abbas II who first clearly realized that Persian painting was in danger of complete stagnation in the Riza tradition and needed an impulse from without if it was to develop renewed creative energy. The best method seemed to him to have talented young men trained in Western workshops, and so he sent some students with stipends to Rome for training. At least one of these full filled his expectations, MUHAMMAD ZAMAN, who has left a number of examples of his work, which show that his study of Italian painting had influenced him without entirely obliterating his Iranian characteristics. Among other paintings are three miniatures that he added to the famous Nizami of Shah Tahmasp, one of which shows Bahram Gur's contest with the dragon, and all of which are dated 1675/6 (10-86 H.). In the same year he painted an illustration of the birth of Rustam and another miniature in *Shah-Nāma* in the collection of A. Chester Beatty, Esq. He appears as a careful and skilful draftsman who had given up the two-dimensional style and used modelled contours and European perspective in his landscapes. Other works by him form the following years are known.[58]

Shah Abbas II was keenly interested to incorporate the Western art-motifs in the Persian miniature painting and the Isfahan centre systematically took its initiative in this direction. Especially the works of the above Persian painter (Muḥammad Zamān) are important to mention here in this regard:

> Abbas II is known to have favoured Western artists, and it was under his reign that the famous Chihil Sutun palace in Isfahan had its walls painted by Dutch painters and their Persian pupils. It was moreover Abbas II who sent the Persian painter Muhammed Zaman to Rome to study Western art. Muḥammad Zaman returned to Persia by 1675 and continued to work in Isfahan at least as late as 1697.[59]

During the times of Shah Abbas II an other skilful draughtsman, Riza's son, Shafi, who was famous for his specialization in **'bird'** and **'flower'** drawing worked till 1674 for the Isfahan School. It is said that after the death of the Shah he left for India to work in the Mughal Court. In the year 1653 he dedicated some of his fine works to the Shah :

> Riza's son Shafi was a tight and careful draughtsman who seems to have specialized in bird and flower drawing, and to have worked as a designer for textiles. The period of his activity seems to have lain mainly within the reign of Shah Abbas II (1642-1667), but he probably survived until 1674, possibly in India, where he may have migrated to the Mughal Court after the death of that Shah. There is a finished drawing of a goldfinch dedicated to the Shah in the year 1653,...[60]

CONCLUSION :

In brief, the Isfahan School of Iranian miniature painting emerged as an important art centre in the 16th and 17th centuries. By the end of the 16th Century Isfahan had become Persia's capital and its contribution to the Iranian art-history is remarkable. Under the patronage of Shah Abbas I and Shah Abbas II this school developed its art-activities. The themes of the miniature paintings comprise the ***Shah Nāmah*** of Shah Abbas I, Riza Abbasi's works, Neo-Timurid manuscripts, Bayunghur's ***Shah Nāmah, Qiṣaṣ al-Anbīyā***, (History of the Prophets) of Nishapuri, ***Khamsa*** *of Nizāmī (addition to some of its previously executed miniature works),* and other many subjects. The influence of Western art is also seen in the last phase of this school.

The prominent Master ***artists*** of the Irfahan school include **Rizā 'Abbāsī** (the chief painter), **Āqā Rizā Murīd** or **Āqā Rizā**, **Mu'in**, **Muḥammad Shafī**.

Mir Afzal Tūnī, Ḥabīb Allah, Malik Ḥusayn, Muḥamamd Yūsuf Al-Ḥusainī, Shah Qāsim, Muḥammad 'Alī and **Muḥammad Zamān** etc.

Some of the *important miniatures* of the school (for our present purpose) are (from *Qiṣaṣal-Anbīyā)* : *Moses and Aaron Conjuring up a Dragon which attacks the Magician Servants of Pharaoh* (by Aqa Riza, 1590-1600); —————————— *Kay Khursau Offering the Crown to Luhrasp,* (1614), [from *Shah Nāmah* of Shah 'Abbās I): *Love Scene* [by Muḥammad Yūsuf al-Husainī (1630)].

REFERENCES

1. Gray, B., *op. cit.*, p. 57.
2. *Treasures of Islam, op. cit.*, p. 48.
3. Sharif, M.M., (edt.) *A History of Muslim Philosophy, op. cit.*, p. 1119.
4. Pope, A.U., *op. cit.*, p. 1844.
5. Norah Titley, "Fourteenth Century Persian Painting : A survey", in (edt.) *Persian Painting : Fourteenth Century* (by M.R. Anand etc.), New Delhi, 1977, p. 58.
6. Pope A.U., op. cit., p. 1841.
7. *Ibid.*, pp. 1845-6.
8. Wilson, R.P., (edt.) *Paintings From Islamic Lands*, Bruno Cassirer, Britain, 1969, p. 84.
9. Gray B., *op. cit.*, pp. 95-100.

10. *Ibid.*, p. 96-103.

11. *Ibid.*, p. 96.

12. *Ibid.*, pp. 104-7.

13. *Ibid.*, p. 540.

14. Norah Titley, "Fourteenth Century Persian Painting", *op. cit.*, p. 58.

15. Gray, B., *op. cit.*, p. 110.

16. *Ibid.*, pp. 189-123.

17. *Ibid.*, p. 109.

18. Bamborough, Philips, *Treasures of Islam* (Book: N), Heritage Pubs., New Delhi, p. 48.

19. *Encyclopedia of the Arts* edited by Dagobert D. Runes & H.G. Schrickel, Philosophical Library, New York, 1946, p. 733.

20. *Treasures of Islam, op. cit.*, p. 48.

21. Gray, B., *Persian Painting, op. cit.*, p. 114.

22. Marg, "Bihzad and the Herat Renaissance" in Mulk Raj Anand & Others (edt.) *Persian Painting : Fifteenth Century*, New Delhi, 1977, p. 03.

23. M. Ajmal, "Painting" in M.M. Sharif's (edt.) *A History of Muslim Philosophy, op. cit.*, pp. 1120-1.

24. *Ibid.*, pp. 33-4.

25. Marg, *op. cit.*, p. 3.

26. Marg, "The Emergence of Style in Fourteenth Century Persian Painting" in *Persian Painting: Fourteenth Century* (by M.R. Anand etc.), 1977, Delhi, p. 6.

27. Anand, M.R., "The Sources of Creative Art in Persia in the Early Medieval Centuries", in *Persian Painting : Fourteenth Century, op. cit.*, p. 15.

28. Pope, A.U., *op. cit.*, p. 1843.

29. Gray, B., *op. cit.*, pp. 24-43.

30. *Ibid.*, pp. 24-5.

31. *Ibid.*, pp. 25-6.

32. Pope, A.U., *op. cit.*, p. 1843.

33. Gray, B., *op. cit.* 28.

34. Pope, A.U., *op. cit.*, pp. 1872-84.

35. Anand, M.R., *Persian Painting : Fifteenth Century., op. cit.*, p. 30.

36. Philip B., *Treasures of Islam, op. cit.*, pp. 48-53.

37. *Ibid.*, p. 53.

38. Pope, A.U., *op. cit.*, p. 1872.

39. Hill, A., (General editor), *A Visual Dictionary of Art, op. cit.*, p. 486.

40. Boyle, J.A. (edt.), *Persia: History and Heritage,* Henry Melland Ltd., London 1978, p. 83.

41. *Ibid,* pp. 83-4.

42. Gray, B., *op. cit.*, p. 142.

43. *Ibid,* p. 145.

44. Hill, A., (editor) *op. cit.*, p. 52.

45. Sharief, M.M., (ed.) *A History of Muslim Philosophy. op.* cit., p. 931.

46. Hill, A., *op. cit.*, P. 314.

47. Gray, B., *op. cit.*, pp. 167-8.

48. *Ibid*, p. 166.

49. Pope, A.U., *op. cit.*, p. 1884.

50. *Ibid.*, p. 1885.

51. *Ibid.*, pp. 1886-7.

52. *Ibid.*, p. 1887.

53. *Ibid.*, p. 1890.

54. Gray, B., *Ibid.*, p. 168.

55. Pope, A.U., *Ibid.*, p. 1896.

56. *Ibid.*, p. 1896.

57. Gray. B., *Ibid.*, p. 168.

58. Pope, A.U. *Ibid.*, pp. 1890-7.

59. Gray, B., *Ibid.*, pp. 168-70.

60. *Ibid.*, p. 168.

CHAPTER V

CONCLUDING REMARKS

(A) Iran's contribution to Islamic Painting
(B) Influence of Iranian Painting on Mughal, Turkish and other Schools of Painting

CHAPTER V

CONCLUDING REMARKS

(A) IRAN'S CONTRIBUTION TO ISLAMIC PAINTING :

Religion has throughout been a source of inspiration for all creative artists and aestheticians of different ages. From the beginning of man's history till date, religion proved itself as a turning point and a unique centre of man's existence. Various art-forms such as **music, sculpture, painting, architecture** and **poetry** etc. have been deeply motivated by intense religious consciousness. In every age and stage religion has helped an artist to create something new with the help of his distinctive spiritual vision. Both religion and art have engraved their everlasting effects on human civilization in ancient, medieval and modern times.

Islam is one of the greatest religions of the world. Its approach to man's life and his spirituality is somewhat different form that of other religions such as Hinduism, Buddhism, Judaisim and Christianity. There is no object or model of the Supreme Reality in Islamic art-world to be painted or portrayed as in case of other religions. However, the consequent 'Void' has its distinctive significance in the Islamic art-world. *Al-Tawhid* (Unity of Being) is the essence of Islam and this metaphysical principle of

Unity is the spiritual significance of the 'Void' which is the only goal and soul of Islamic art. **Allah** is not seen like an object but He is realized as the Supreme Creator and Sustainer of everything. He has bestowed upon man the power of wisdom and creativity.

The independence and originality of Islamic art can directly be traced from its specific world-view. There is an indispensable relation between the Islamic revelation and Islamic art. God is the source of all and He is the Knower of all things. Therefore, the essences or forms of all things have their reality in the Divine Intellect.

We have already tried to highlight some most important Islamic art-forms in general, and Iranian contribution to Islamic art in particular, to understand the essence of Islamic art-world. Generally, the work of art, as we know, is an organised complex of sensuous and expressive elements, and its organisation is its form. But in Islamic art man's spiritual dimension has been overemphasized. All art and thought have been derived form this very emphasis. According to Sayyed Hossein Nasr, it is in reality "the inner dimension of Islam, to the *baṭin* as contained in the way and elucidated by the Truth, that one, must turn for the origin of Islamic art. This inner dimension is moreover inextricably related to Islamic spirituality."[1]

The art of Islam is Islamic art not because it was created by Muslims but because it issues forth from the Islamic revelation as do the Divine Law and the Way. This art crystallizes in the world of forms the inner realities of the Islamic revelation, and issues from the inner dimension of Islam revealing to man the Ultimate *Sanctum - Sanctorum* of Divine Revelation. In brief, Islamic art is a fruit of Islamic spirituality from the point of view of its genesis and as an aid. It is a complement and support for the spiritual life from the vantage point of realization or return to the Origin—the *summum bonum* of human life.

In brief, Islamic art is the result of the manifestation of Unity upon the plane of multiplicity. It reflects in its own distinctive manner the Unity of the Divine Principle— the dependence of all multiplicity upon the One-**Allah**. This art makes manifest, in the physical order directly perceivable by the senses, the archetypal realities and acts. Therefore, it is a ladder for the journey of the soul form the audio-visual world to the Invisible which is also silence transcending all sound.

To grasp the above true spirit of the Islamic art as well as its spiritual significance, we shall have to through further a bird's eye view over the main contributions of Iran to Islamic art, particularly painting.

In different art-forms such as **calligraphy, miniature painting, music, poetry** and other **minor** or **plastic arts** in general, the contribution of Iran to the Islamic arts is commendable. Though we have already discussed the Iranian influence on Islamic Art in the *second* and the *third* chapters of this project, here in addition to that, we shall briefly describe some more points regarding Islamic art in general and painting in particular. Since the advent of Islam, we find that the elements of creative activity has got much value and importance in Islamic world. The categorical fine arts have all been practised in characteristic manner by Islamic people. Muslim artists did not consider any distinction between fine and useful arts. But it is a fact that during the early stage of Islam, art-activity was undeveloped though aesthetic sensibility was inherent in Muslim artists.

So far as the Iranian contribution to Islamic art is concerned we can simply point out that throughout the long centuries of Islamic history one of the major inspiring powerful forces of Islamic civilization and especially art has been Persia. If we substrate or ignore Persia from Islamic art or Islamic cultural history everything would remain incomplete. The traditional miniature painting, architechture, ceramic, designs in decorating buildings, roofs, walls, gates etc., and the different Persian motifs in the field of art, left an everlasting effect on Islamic aesthetics. Because a tradition embraces all of man's life and activities, so after embracing Islam, Iranian people made a radical attempt to Islamize all forms of art. Henceforth, the **'traditional'** and the **'sacred'** both art-forms went together. Both are indispensable yet not indentical as well :

> It must first of all be remembered that 'traditional' and 'sacred' are inseparable, but not identical. The quality termed

> 'traditional' pertains to all the manifestations of a traditional civilization reflecting the spiritual principles of that civilization both directly and indirectly. 'Sacred', however, especially as used in the case of art, must be reserved for those traditional manifestations which are directly connected with the spiritual principles in question, hence with religious and initiatic rites and acts possessing a sacred subject and a symbolism of a spiritual character. Opposed to the sacred stands the profane and opposed to the traditional, the anti-traditional.[2]

It is undoubtedly the greatness of the Persian people who actively imbibed the Islamic principles with their traditional art-activity and contributed a lot to **'Islamic Art'**. Persian people applied the principles of Islamic revelation in the creation of numerous outstanding forms of Islamic art. Seyyed Ḥossein Nasr writes in this regard :

> Persia, where the principles of the sacred art of Islam in relation to spirituality can be demonstrated amply in many fields and domains of art, both plastic and sonoral. Persian art, at once deeply Persian and Islamic, represents a culmination of Islamic art and one of its indisputable peaks. The highly artistic nature of Persian and their love for beauty, refinement, and delicacy enabled them not only to create one of the great schools of art in the ancient world associated with the Achaemenians. Parathions and Sesamoids, but also to absorb and apply the principles of Islamic revelation in the creation of numerous outstanding works of Islamic art. Both because of its richness, variety, and depth of expression. Persian Islamic art presents an ideal field for the study of the sacred art of Islam in relation to Islamic spirituality on the one hand and to the ethos and genius of a particular people and culture on the other.[3]

In order to understand more clearly the Iranian contribution to Islamic Art, it seems desirable to present a brief survey of some of the most important Islamic art-forms particularly **'painting'**. In their connection we shall take up mainly : (1) *Calligraphy*, (2) *Miniature Painting* :

(A) CALLIGRAPHY :

Regarding calligraphy Imam 'Alī ibn Abī Ṭālib once said : ***"The beauty of writing is the tongur of the hand and the elegance of thought."*** As we have stated earlier (in the Third Chapter of this thesis) that the Arabic script had a metaphysical or spiritual significance in Islamic culture. The **'Word'** of ***Allah*** has spiritual importance for the Muslims and therefore, the followers of Islam took the great interest in this field of art. 'Arabic' being the religious language of Muslims provided a common platform for the believers of Islamic faith and tradition. The Arabic script, which is written from right to left, is the most widely used language in the Middle East. The Holy Qur'ān teaches love and brotherhood in Islam with no discrimination among peoples of different races, regions or colour, and the Arabic has achieved this important goal by providing a common understanding and inter-communication. The Arabic script became a language or medium of spiritual relation in Islam :

> One of the visible links of Islam that can be seen throughout the Islamic world, in countries of different races and cultural backgrounds, is the Arabic script. The use of Arabic in the religion is an essential part of Islam, for its acts as a religious bond, drawing peoples together with a common religious language, in much the same way a Latin was used in the early

> Christian church. Infact, the parallel goes further both Latin and Arabic were the languages used by the original followers of Christianity and Islam respectively. The Qur'an teaches brotherhood in Islam with no discrimination between men of different races and colour. Arabic has helped to achieve this by providing a common platform and language of inter-communication. So successful had this been that over the last thirteen hundred years there have been more books written in Arabic in non-Arab countries than in Arab countries. The use of common religious language has helped keep the forces of regionalism and nationalism, at bay, which have many times threatened to break up the Islamic world. Arabic has given spiritual identity, a universal cosmopolitan entity and real meaning to Islam.[4]

When we look at the Persian's contrubution to this important form of Islamic Art we find that this form flourished in its best manner in Iran. Though the Arabs had great love for their language, yet they could not make it a separate significant Islamic art-form. The credit goes to the Persian people in general and artists in particular who took their keen interest in this field and widely used and still using it different fields of aesthetics such as **architechture, painting** and other **decorative arts**. The Arabic script was also adopted for Persian, Turkish, Urdu and most other languages used by Muslims. Therefore, in most of the Islamic Art-forms Arabic and its allied languages became the significant decorative motif :

> The Islamic holy book, called the Qur'ān and non-religious writings often appear on the wall of religious buildings and on art objects. These writings, in variuos styles, are beautifully executed. Sometimes they are combined with floral or geometric designs, but only rarely with animal or human figures.[5]

The Arabic alphabet was written mainly in **four** distinct styles namely *Kūfic, Naskhi, Nasta'līq* and *Shikasta*. The Kufic script received its name from the city of Kūfah (Iraq). It is said that the first copies of the Holy Qur'ān were written in this script. "The Kufic form of the script emerged as the most import of several variants"[6] especially by the 8th century. The most celebrated masters of the Abbasid period were Khoshnam of Basra, al-Mehdī of Kūfah[7] and the Baghdad calligrapher, Abū 'Alī Muḥammad.

Nasikhi, a round script, was the characteristic writing of the Seljuq period. The Master calligraphers was Muḥammad ibn Khāzin of Dinawar, Yāqūt of Mosul and 'Abdullah Sairafī. The greatest later Master was Hafiz 'Usmān in the late 17th century.[8] Various **miniature paintings** were executed centeralizing calligraphic themes.

Nasta 'līq, (the combination of the two earlier Arabic scripts : *'Naskhi'* and *'ta'līq'*) emerged as the dominant Arabic writing in the *Fārs* (Iran) soil. Iranian calligraphers, since the late 14th century, tried to developed this script with great innovation and religious zeal. The contribution of the Persian calligraphers to this important Islamic art-form is undoubtedly remarkable :

> Nasta'liq the most completely Persian of the forms, with a drooping ductus, strongly repetitive curvature, and an almost complete elimination of straight lines, evolves gradually in

> the late 14th and early 15th Cent. Master : Mir 'Ali Tabrizi its "inventor", the Timurid Prince Baysunghur (inscriptions in the mosque of Gawhar Shad, Mashhad), Ja'far Tabrizi (Tehran Shahnama of 1430), later masters, represented in most of the great collections of mss., are : Sultan 'Akli Mashhadi, his son Sultan Muhammad Nur, Shah Mahmud Nishapuri, Mir 'Ali Harawi, the great master of album-pieces (mashq) Mir 'Imadal Hasani, and his rival the designer of many of the Is'fahan building inscriptions, 'Ali Riza 'Abbasi.[9]

Briefly we can say that Persian contributed a lot in this important form of Islamic Art. The Arabic calligraphy in particular, and Persian, Turkish and Urdu in general were the languages of great importance for Muslim. Arabic is the common language of both the Holy Qur'an and *Salat* (ritual prayers). Therefore, the religious ritual also is both understood personally and universally throughout the world of Islam. Thus, the Arabic calligraphy has a spiritual significance and the Iranian artists or calligraphers executed this script in different styles. The art of calligraphy (in Arabic and other allied languages) was flourished in Iran and with constant striving of her master artists reached its zenith. **(See Plate 2 , 3,4 , 19).**

The Qur'ān, the **Word** of ***Allah*** and the calligraphy. the hand of man. got religious values and importance. It is a sacred art in Muslim world. The Holy Qur'ān is link between the Arabic script and Islamic world. It was regarded not as the written account of the Prophet's teachings but as the very **"word"** of ***Allah***. Iranian calligraphers applied this important Islamic art for to fields such as architechture, painting, decorative arts etc. A good hand-writing was considered as a symbol of purity, good culture and disciplined mind of soul. Briefly, we can say that the Islamic calligraphy has the spiritual message to convey :

> It has become identified over the centuries with culture itself, good calligraphy being taken as a sign of a cultured man and a disciplined mind and soul as well as hand. Calligraphy has continued to be the central visual art with its numerous applications ranging from architecture to poetry. Calligraphy is the basic art of creation of points and lines in an endless variety of forms and rhythms which never cease to bring about recollection (*tidhkar* or *dhikr*) of the Primordial Act of the Divine Pen for those who are capable of contemplating in forms the trace of the formless.[10]

As there is no object or model of the Supreme Reality (***Allah***) in Islamic world to be painted or portrayed as in case of other religions. So the Muslim artists prepared **painting** on the symbolic representation of 'nature' and the like. The Arabic script, particlarly, the Qur'anic Veses as well as Persian, Urdŭ and Turkish languages and literature became the subject-matter for the Islamic paintings. Iran has contributed a lot in this form of Islamic art. **(See Plate 28).**

(B) MINIATURE PAINTING :

Iran has long been famous for her architecture, poetry and painting. Traditional Persian painting features delicate detail work and jewel-like colours. Iranian painters tried to reform and re-establish the Muslim attitude towards painting. According to them painting was no longer the art of '**making images**' but, in reality, it was the art of '**breaking images**': "Through painting one could now cast out the devils of one's heart and thus prepare one's soul for direct encounter with God. There was no longer any question of worshipping the gods one painted, for no longer did they remain to objects of worship for the Muslim mind."[11] It is this fact that Muslim painters began to pay attention towards painting.

Muslim artists in general and Iranian in particular do realize that Islam itself inherited the profound **aesthetic** possibilities. They further do understand that Islam encourages the **creative** aspect of man to unfold the inner aesthetic potentiality. Muslim painting was only an aspect of Muslim life. The Iranian artists hold that painting was an expression of the spiritual exploration of sensitive minds: "These sensitive minds, rooted in their own culture, had their own peculiar longings and yearnings, aspirations and conflicts. It was out of these dynamic forces that peculiar idioms and patterns of artistic expression were evolved. It is these idioms and patterns which we call by the name of Muslim Art."[12]

Iran gave her remarkable contribution to Islamic Art in general and painting in particular. In their paintings. Iranian artists employed symbols which represent the mystical states. They portrayed different aspects of **nature** in their miniature painting because of the fact that they regarded every aspect and object of **nature** as manifestation of ***Allah*** :

> Muslim painting, especially in Iran, was devoted to the expression of a single emotion in one painting. Every detail of the subject was perceived and made use of for an effective rendering of the subtle nuances of that emotion. The trees and flowers were not there to fill a background ; they were there to add to the melody flowing from a painting. Most of the Persian miniature Paintings are like orchestres in which each object painted contributes to the symphony. This unique characteristic of Muslim painting may have emanated—as Basil Gray suggests—from the mystical and pantheistic tendencies of the Persians ; they, perhaps, regarded every object of nature as manifesting God.[13]

A detailed discussion regarding Iranian miniature painting was already taken up by us in the **IV Chapter** (*Schools of Iranian Painting*) of this project, so here it seems desirable to pin-point that the inner desire of Iranians to establish various schools of miniature painting was in reality, a significant contrubution to Islamic Art, especially painting. Muslim paintings specifically miniatures in Iran, are illustrations of literary and religious classics. In almost all the miniature-art the denominate characteristic had been **"nature"** which, according to the Persian painters, was itself an illustration of ***Allah***.

> Several explanations of this peculiar characteristic have been advanced. But the only explanation which is consistent with the general Muslim attitude is that for a Muslim nature is itself an illustration of the Word of God *Kun fa-yakūn* are the words which translate themselves in the sensible world.[14]

As we have already mentioned that in Persian art of painting the chief purpose was to illustrate the literary, ethical and religious or mythological works. In this art the same theme reappear time and again. The works of great Persian Poets and creative writers such Niẓāmī, Firdaūsī, Sa'adī, Jāmī, Hāfiz, Khwāju Kirmānī, al-Birūnī, Mīr 'Alī Shir Nawāi, Amir Khusrraū (of Delhi), Muhyi Lārī, Rashd al-Dīn, and so on, became the subject-matter for the Persian painters like Bihzād, Āqā Mīrāk, Āqā Rizā 'Abbāsī, 'Abdullah, Abd al-Razzāq, Abd al-Ṣamad, Aḥmad Mūsā, Dūst Muḥammad, Muḥammadī, Mīr Sayyīd 'Alī, Mīr 'Alī Tabrīzī, Ḥabib Allah, Muḥammad Yūsuf al-Ḥusaynī, Shah Qāsim, Muḥammad 'Alī, Muḥammad Zamān, Mu'īn etc. These and thousand other prominent artists under the patronage of different Persian Kings or ***Sultans*** executed and produced masterpieces in miniature-art and their this contribution to different Islamic art-forms (particularly painting) made the Islamic art as a significant aspect of Islamic *Weltanschauung*. It is said that "one of the greatest strengths of Islamic art has always been its ability to absorb so many different traditions and yet retain its vital individuality."[15] It is the greatness of Iran which tried to maintain the **spiritual significance** of Islamic art in the **creative activity** of human being.

(B) INFLUENCE OF IRANIAN PAINTING ON MUGHAL, TURKISH AND OTHER SCHOOLS OF PAINTING :

(i) Influence on Mughal School :

Mughal art, in its true spirit, has rightly been indebted to Iranian art-tradition. In every art-form executed under the Mughal Kings and art-lovers it seems quite clear that colour scheme, technique, perspective and style of representation etc., everything has the Iranian influence. The styles and techniques of various schools of Persian art left remarkable impact on the Mughal art and thought. In architecture as well as in the art of miniature painting the Herat, Tabriz and Shiraz styles can suitably be mentioned here :

> The Palette is rich and varied, brushstrokes are delicate (stippling finds little place before Late Mughal Painting) ; the view point is regularly high, to show both exterior and interior of buildings, and the perspective may depend on different vanishing-points at different levels of the picture. The Persian side of its ancestry is shown in the Herat-style tiled floors and walls, cypress tress laced by creeping flowering plants, and especially the persistent red rail-fences ; features of the Shiraz style sometimes appear in the landscape. Under Akbar the paintings are often by more than one artist. The work of master artists was copied by tracings which were than pricked along the essential lines and used for copying by pouncing charcoal through ; this was employed not only to train young artists but also by the masters to copy their own details; old tracings might be used in later reigns to copy portraits of earlier rulers. With the development of the muraqqas under Jahangir, paintings of different sizes are accommodate : in uniform album pagers by elaboration of the *hashiya* (border); here the designs have affinities with those of bookbinding and those of architectural panels and dadoes.[16]

The Mughal Emperors were much inspired by the Persian art because of the fact that their ancestors had deep love for art and literature and their immense aesthetic urged compelled them to visit different Persian art-centres. As we all know, inspired by the Persian art Mughal

Sultans introduced a new type of painting which bears their name. They descended form Tīmūr (popularly known as Tamerlane) who was a Turk from Central Asia. He sacked Delhi in 1394 but his descendents conquered India only in the 16th Century A.D. Although a despot, Tīmūr patronised poets, musicians and other thinkers in Samarkhand, which was his Capital. During the rule of his son Shah Rukh, we have the first record of support given by him to painters or artists. At the end of the 15th century A.D. Tīmūr's power diminished and the Safavid Kings got the reign who ruled with much splendour at Tabriz, then a famous centre of learning and art. Here a brilliant school of Persian painting developed and the best talented artists were engaged to work on book-illustration for the royalty.[17]

Babur, a descendent of Tīmūr, also inherited his ancestor's love for the arts. His aesthetic sensibility motivated him to visit Herat, the capital of Tīmūr's son, Shah Rukh. Herat was the centre of art and Islamic culture where Bābur saw the famous painting of the Masters painter Bhizād and his followers. Thus during the four years of his rule in India (1526-1530) Bābur longed for the familiar artistic spelndour of the Herat School of Persian painting.[18]

Humāyūn (1530-1556) inherited his father's deep artistic inclination. But due to political uncertainty he could not do much in this field. When he was driven into exile by the Afghān usurper Shēr Shah Sūr in 1540 he took refuge at the court of the Persian Safavid ruler, Shah Tahmasp, where he could admire the collection of illuminated manuscripts and observe minutely the artists at work. The Shah helped him in establishing a small court in Kabul in 1550 and the Chief painters like Mīr Muṣawwir, Mīr Sayyīd 'Alī, 'Abd-al-Ṣamad were invited form Iran for miniature painting and book - illustrations.[19] In this connection it seems desirable to mentioned the illustrated work of the story of Amīr Ḥamza which is popularly known as *Ḥamza Nāmah*. Under the Patronage of Humāyūn this work was beautifully executed by the master Persian painters :

> This school of painting owes its genesis to the patronage extended by emperor Humāyūn (1530-1556) to the two Persian artists of Shiraz, Mīr Sayyaīd 'Alī and Abdus Ṣamad. They remained in India as the court painters of Humayun. they executed their work in the manner of the Persian Safavid School. Humayun commissioned these artists to illustrate the work of *Ḥamzanāmah* or the story of Amīr Ḥamza. This was a colossal undertaking and was completed in twelve volumes of hundred illustrations each. This work took several years and was only completed during the reign of Akbar who succeeded Humāyūn.[20]

At Kabul both 'Abd al-Ṣamad of Shiraz and Mīr Sayyīd 'Alī of Tabriz were the drawing teachers of Humāyūn's son, little Akbar : "Both mir Sayyīd 'Alī and Khwāja 'Abd-us-Ṣamad were given good positions and appointed painting instructors to young Akbar."[21] Thus, it can be said that this Mughal Emperor Humāyūn, under whose patronage the work of art in Kabul was started –was deeply motivated by the Iranian spirit and style of art and produced mastrerspieces in this field.

Akbar (1556-1605) became the real founder of the Mughal School of painting and it was his creative mind and rich aesthetic sensibility that he established art-centre which bear the name of "**Mughal**". "By 1570 he ruled an extensive and prosperous empire and built a new capital, Fatheḥpur Sīkrī, as well as the fortress of Agra. Around him he gathered administrators, generals, artists, poets and musicians of high calibre and pre-eminence in the respective fields".[22]

King Akbar took extraordinary personal interest in the religion and way of life of his Hindū subjects. Therefore, in order to make his Persian and Turkish administrators and painters well acquainted with Indian concepts, he had the Hindu epics and religious texts translated into Persian and beautifully illustrated as well. It is said that Akbar gave steady employment to about one hundred and fifty artists to work for the illustrations of manuscripts like the ***Ḥamza Nāmah, Chingīz Nāmah***, the ***Ẓafar Nāmah***, the ***Razam Nāmah*** (***Mahābhārātā***), the ***Ramāyane***, ***Nāla- Damayāntī***, the ***Bābur Nāmah***, the ***Akbar Nāmah***, ***Tārkh-i-Alfī*** (history of the world) ***Jāmial-Tawārīkh*** (history of the Mongols by Rashid al-Dīn), ***Tīmūr Nāmah***, and the illustrations of the classical Persian literature such as Niẓām's ***Khamsa***, Sa'adī's ***Gulistān***, Ḥāfiz's ***Dīwān***, Jāmī's Baharistān.[23] In addition to these manuscripts, a large collection of portraits, palace-scenes, hunting scenes, natural objects and bird studies also became the subject-matter of the Mughal school of painting established especially under the able guidance of emperor Akbar.

Akbar was considered a very far-sighted, tolerant, cultural ruler as well as a symbol of Hindu-Muslim composite culture :

> Fortunately for India, Akbar himself was deeply interested in painting, in the religious and in the ancient wisdom of India. For the first time in the course of several centuries of Muslim rule in India, the culture and learning of India found an honourable place in the highest circle of Muslim rulers of India, which was not only brought about a rapprochement between the Hindu and the Muslim but was extremely faithful in evolving a composite culture.[24]

Almost all the Mughal emperors (form Tīmūr to Shah Jahān) were mostly inspired by the Iranian art-tradition. Particularly in the illustrations of the above manuscripts, we find that the whole style, technique, treatment etc. are Persian in tone and spirit. In reality, the traditional school of Indian painting with the traditional art and skill of the Persian school culminated in the shape of **Mughal school of Painting :** "It was during this alchemic age of Akbar's rule that the Persian painting at the court of Humāyūn was transformed into the Indio-Persian art of the Mughal school."[25]

The Mughal emperors (particularly Humāyūn, Akbar and Jahāngīr) patronaized the Mughal school and a number of miniature paintings were produced mainly by the Persian painters or under their supervision. The chief painters were Mīr Sayyīd 'Alī,'Abd-al-Samad (who was already in the service of Humāyūn) and a Hindū painter, Bashawān. In brief, the Master Persian painters like Sayyīd 'Alī and others trained the artists on Persian pattern in order to get the best results in the field of miniature painting :

> Mir Sayyid Ali and Abd-al-Samad drilled the craftsmen in all the technical details of Persian miniatures. Many Indian such as Bashawan, Miskina and Daswanth attained great positions as court artists and 'Abu'l Fazl in his Āin-i Akbarī (biography of Akbar) bestows high praise on them....
>
> Under the supervision of Mīr Sayyīd 'Alī and 'Abd-al-Ṣamad the imperial atelier of painters and calligraphers took shape. Their first endeavour was to complete the pictures for the earliest Mughal illustrated manuscript, the Dastan-i-Amir Hamza (South Kensington and Vienna Museums). Begun in 1550 under Humayun, it took twenty five years to finish. All of the 1375 paintings, however, show consistency in style because Mīr Sayyīd 'Alī had from the start planned out the whole work in the Safavid style, though other artists, either Persian or Indian, assisted him in the actual painting.[26]

Briefly, we can conclude that Iranian paintings have great influence on the Mughal school of miniature art. All the illustrations of the Mughal school followed the Persian Safavid mode or style — a two-dimensional, realistic, decorative way of painting without shading or perspective, well suitable for manuscripts and excellent use of calligraphic line-drawing filled with enamel-like colours, usually hilly landscapes with a lofty horizon formed the background of the pictures seem prominent. Persian artists and Kings had much love for **'nature'** and thus, we find **the element** of nature in every piece of art, especially in miniature painting. **The Persian** trends and techniques constantly became a source of inspiration for the Mughal school of Painting :

> Although the Persian school of painting gave a vast stimulus to the birth of the Mughal, its influence did not last. Indians learned from it the use of brilliant colours and refinement of lines. In the animal representations, the Indian genius manifested itself with that intimate knowledge and love which characteristics it.[27]

Hence, the style of drawing and painting introduced into Indian sub-continent by the Mughal ***Sulṭāns*** from the early 16th century onwards was essentially and avowedly Persian. It is due to this Persian influence that the Mughal School is sometimes also called as **"Indo-Persian School of Painting"**. In the field of miniature painting or portraiture this Indo-Persian school has got its unique place in all Asiatic schools of art : "The special glory of the Indo-Persian school, distinguishing it above all other schools of Asiatic art, is its high attainment in portraiture".[28] In respect of creative activity of the Mughal school, the impact of Persian spirit in undoubtedly great and inspiring. **(See Plate 5, 8 , 18).**

(ii) Influence of Iranian Painting on Turkish and other schools

In the previous section we have briefly discussed the Iranian influence on the Mughal arts' particular painting. In the similar way

Iranian art-tradition left its remarkable impact in the Turkish and other schools of painting.

So far as the origin and development of Turkish painting is concerned, no autrhentic literature or evidence is still known. "Turkish painting is still wrapped in mystery."[29] However, this much we find that during 855/1480 Sulṭān Muḥammad II invited Getile Bellini[30] (Venetian painter and son of Jacopo Belline, the Master painter)[31] to his court and commissioned him to paint his portrait. Thus, we see that the European elements began to enter the great stream of Islamic art, because painter like Gentile Bellini visited Istanbūl to paint the portrait of the Sulṭān, and the Turkish artists, in return, paid visit to Europe.

Generally, it is accepted that Ottoman school of painting was started in the second half of the 15th century and it got its due recognition during the 16th century A.D. The Saray library in Istanbūl has the collection of the arts of the Ottoman Turks of the 16th century which clearly provide an evidence of the establishment of the Turkish School of painting :

> One such instance is well illustrated by a large number of paintings that have mainly been preserved in albums in the Saray Library in Istanbul ; and other paintings related to those can usually be found to have been at one time in the collections of the Sultans of Turkey. The fact that so many of these paintings are preserved in the Saray and that parallels can be found in the arts of the Ottoman Turks if the 16th century, led the writer to conclude that these represent a "School of Turkish painting".[32]

But it is only partially true about the Turkish school. The researchers, on the basis of their close study, pointed out that the 'Turkish School' of art or painting is an out-come of the various styles, most prominently the Persian:

> This is only partially true and now after five years of detailed study of the entire material, it has become clear that the "Turkish School" is only one manifestation of the style. The style itself is indigenous neither to Turkey nor to any other specific place in the Islamic world ; rather, it seems to have developed while travelling possibly form Samarqand and Herat to Tabriz and finally to Istanbul. In fact the possible connection of the Turkish phase of the style, with a centre of painting on the east had already been recognized when the first survey of the material was made, but only now does it seem possible to establish what then was supposition.[33]

Again, it has sometimes been assumed that the Turks as a race have made but little contribution to the field of art. But it is a fact that whatever they have created was mostly under the influence of Iranian art-tradition. "... the quality of works produced under their patronage is to be attributed to that they employed Persian, Armemian of Greek craftmen."[34]

In the 16th century A.D. the two famous master painters of Iran namely Shah Qulī and Walī Jan came to Constantiople and became Turkish Court painter. These renowned painters illustrated ***the History of the Ottoman Sulṭāns, Sulaimān Nāmah*** and, in addition to these works, they have selected **'houris of paradise'** as their subject-matter :

> These artists selected the houris of paradise as their subject-matter. Shah Qulī achieved excellence as a painter of curved, leaves and Walī Jan became distinguished for the elegance of his lines. Some Iranian painters illustrated "History of the Ottoman Sultans" and Sulaiman Nameh, a book of stories by Firdausi of Brusa. The main distinction of these painters was that they did a good deal of experimental work in colours.[35]

Turkish school of painting is essentially provincial and throughout the 16th century Persian artists continued to command highly over the Turkish artists and contributed a lot in the development of Turkish art and architechture. In this connection the artists from Herat and Tabriz deserve special mention over here.

Osman was one of the most important Turkish painter who too was much inspired by the Persian technique and style and beautifully illustrated historical manuscript called ***Huner Nāmah*** for the Ottoman Court. The Book was written in Persian by Luqmān bin Ḥuseyn and describes events during the reign of King Sulēymān :

> The 'Book of Accomplishments' was written in Persian by the Ottoman historian Luqmān b. Ḥuseyn al-only one 'Ashurī, in the second half of the 16th century. It describes events in the reign of sultan Sulēymān (1520-66), and is illustrated with miniatures which are attributed to the Turkish painter, Osman.[36]

Another famous Turkish painter, besides Osman, was Āmīn al-Khalāfa. They (Osman and Āmīn) have produced a series of portraits of the Ottoman Sultans. Most of the great Turkish masterpieces in the field of miniature art are in the various libraries of Istanbūl and they are still unknown to the West. Both the artists got profound perfection in Persian pattern intorduced especially by the Persian Masters, Shah-Qulī and Walī Jān.[37]

However, it is also a fact that the quality of Turkish Islamic paining has been under-estimated for a long time. No doubt, the Turkish art of painting is a provincial offshoot of the great Persian tradition of book-illustration or book-illumination, yet this art has its own identity which is inherent in its unique style and colour-scheme :

> This is certainly not so, despite occasional technical and stylistic derivations from Persian miniatures. Turkish painting has a very bold and specific style of its own characterised by a preference for historical subject-matter, a general emphasis on the realistic detail and by extremely bold compositions based on primary colours.[38]

Sharing the similar view-point about the Turkish painting, Philip Bamborough beautifully explains the main difference between the Persian miniature-art and the Turkish one in the following words :

> Although influenced by the Persian miniature tradition. Turkish painting is quite different. There is always an indigenous element which marks it as "Turkish". Apart from the obvious differences in costume, there is a difference in the landscape which accurately reflects the somewhat austere nature of the terrain. The colours, too, differ as well as the use of gold and silver. Whereas the colours in Persian paintings are subtle and delicate. those in Turkish paintings tend to be stronger and a little harsh, with shades of blue, green, purple. and red predominating. The paintings are in keeping with Islamic

> tradition and like the Persian avoid atmospheric effects and optical illusions. Turkish paintings are to a great extent reportage of historical and sacred events. Whereas Persian paintings tend to be romantic interpretations of pottery, myth the history. The Turkish painter was a master of crowd scenes, which he recorded with vivid realism and detail. At first, as the Turks were fond of military expeditions, many of the paintings recorded battle scenes, victories and triumphal processions. Later, with a decline in military activity, painters concentrated on festivals and important social events.[39]

But the famous Turkish art historian 'Alī points out that most Turkish miniatures are unsigned and even where they are signed, the authenticity of the signature is somewhat dubious. Therefore, we cannot rely upon such paintings to tell us much. 'Alī records that in the 16th century Agha (or Āqā) Mīrāk, the master Persian painter from Tabriz come to Turkey in the reign of Sulaymān. Another artist, also form Tabriz, was Velican. From this information of 'Alī it can rightly be inferred that there were many non-Turkish artists who worked in Turkey for the Sultans.[40] We have already mentioned that during the same period (16th century) two other great artists Shah Qulī and 'Alī Jān executed various beautiful miniatures for the Turkish Kings. Thus, we can conclude that though Turkish School of miniature painting has got in it the elements form Europe and Far East yet the overwhelming influence over the entire school is of Persia :

> Perhaps the most interesting information in 'Alī's account is the large number of non-Turkish artists who worked in Turkey,

> **a fact which accounts for the cosmopolitan quality of Turkish painting. The predominant foreign influence was Persian, but there were also many others. The earliest Turkish painting is influenced by the Persian Herat style, and the later painting of the 16th and 17th century by the Safavid style. Some influence from Europe and the Far East, in particular Italy and china, was also felt.[41] (See Plate 32).**

In the end, so for as the Iranian influence on the other schools of painting is concerned, we can briefly say that sepecially in Indian context, there has been a continuous Persian elements found prominently in the provincial Mughal schools situated mainly in Lucknow, Faizabad, Murshidabad, Hyderabad and Oudh.[42]

In the Deccani Islamic painting, under Bahmanis—especially in Bidar, Berar, Ahmednagar, Bijapur and Golconda—the rulers were of Persian or Afghan in origin who patronized distinctive architectural styles besides encouraging painting and music. For example, Sultan Ḥusaīn Niẓām Shah I of Aḥmadnagar was very much found of the Persian art-motifs. After his death his widow commissioned the illustrated manuscript in praise of his valour. This work called ***Tārīf-i-Ḥussaīn Shahī*** in which we clearly find the Persian elements.[43]

In the Rajput painting (in its *two* styles : the Rājasthānī and the Pahārī school) we find that in direct or indirect manner. the Persian influence appears great. The Rajasthani schools, which flourished between the 16th and early 19th centuries in different feudal states. one can easily find the Mughal or Persian styles. From the view-point of painting the most important Rajasthani schools such as Mewar, Bundi, Jaipur, Kishangarh and Kotah owed much in them from the Mughal and the Persian techniques. In this connection the Mewar miniatures namely ***The Meeting of the Poet with his Beloved*** and ***Ragmala Series*** are important to mention here. The commissioning of Muslim artists by the Hindu patrons and vice-versa was quite common in those days. The Muslim or Hindu artists were trained by the Persian Masters artists in the Mughal court and subsequently, these painters worked and produced miniature paintings under Persian art-tradition and inspiration. In Jaipur, Jodhpur, Kotah the Mughal influence (though it is little) but also there, and as we know, the Mughal art-style is chiefly inspired by the Persian.[44]

Again, in Pahari painting, which include the work of different states and their schools, of which the most important were Basohli, Guler, Jammu, Kangra, and Garhwal, also imbibed the basic elements of the Mughal or Persian technique. Briefly, we can say that in all the above schools the Mughal or Persian influence was overwhelming. (See Plate 6,7).

Apart form these schools of Indian art, we see the Iranian influence on schools belonging to other art-loving countries.

GENERAL CONCLUSION OF THE UNDERTAKEN PROJECT :

Iran, being one of the ancient centers of art and culture, has had a rich heritage and has made specific contribution to the enrichment of various Islamic art-forms. Although Iran is best known for its contribution to poetry, yet the contribution to graphic arts can be deemed to be second to none. Iranian art-forms have been basically inspired by Islamic World-view and value-system. Its architechture, music, poetry, calligraphy and painting reflect the inner glory and strength of Islamic Revelation. Various schools have been inspired by this basic vision and they have made excellent contributions to the promotions of various art-forms. The painting has received special attention by some of the distinguished centres of excellence. Some schools such as Shiraz, Herat, Tabriz, Qazwin, Isfahan can be specifically mentioned in this regard ; wherein the art-form of painting has reached its zenith. These schools and various other ones of painting have had widespread impact on non-Iranian schools of painting. Specially of Mughal and Turkish Schools of painting have been deeply inspired by Iranian art-tradition.

REFERENCES

1. Naṣr, S. Ḥ., *Islamic Art and Spirituality, op. cit.*, p. 5-6.
2. *Ibid.*, pp. 65-6.
3. *Ibid.*, p. 64.
4. Bomborough, p., *op. cit.*, p. 21.
5. *The World Book Encyclopedia, op. cit.*, p. 468.
6. Wilson E., *Islamic Designs, op. cit.*, p. 11.
7. Runes. D.D., & Schrickel(ed.) *Encyclopedia of the Arts, op. cit.*, p. 486.
8. *Ibid.*, p. 486.
9. *Ibid.*, pp. 486-7.
10. Naṣr, S. Ḥ., *op. cit.*, p. 19.
11. Ajmal, M., "Painting in M. M. Sharif's(ed.) *A History of Muslim Philosophy, op. cit.*, pp. 1110-1.
12. *Ibid.*, p. 1111.
13. *Ibid.*, p. 1114.
14. *Ibid.*, p. 1115.
15. Hill, A., *A Visual Dictionary of Art, op. cit.*, p. 52.
16. *Ibid.*, p. 421.
17. Tomory. E., p. 250.

18. *Ibid.*, p. 250.

19. *Ibid.*, p. 251.

20. Iyer, K.B., *Indian Art : A Short Introduction*, Asia Publishing House, Bombay, 1958, p. 74.

21. Dās, Asok K., *Dawn of Mughal Painting*, Vikils, Feffer & Simons Ltd., Bombay, 1982, p. 3.

22. Tomory, E., *op. cit.*, p. 251.

23. *Ibid.*, p. 76, and Edith Tomory, *op. cit.*, pp. 251-2.

24. Dās, A. K., *op. cit.*, p. 74-5.

25. Iyer, K. B., *op. cit.*, p. 75.

26. Tomory, E., *op. cit.*, pp. 251-2.

27. *Ibid*, p. 252.

28. Smith, Vincet A., *A History of Fine Art in India and Ceylon*, The Clarendon Press, Oxford, 1911, p. 496.

29. Sharīf, M. M., *op. cit.*, p. 1122.

30. *Ibid.*, p. 1122.

31. Hill, A.. *op. cit.*, pp. 107-8.

32. Wilson. R. P. (ed.) *Painting from Islamic Lands*. Bruno, Cassirer. Britain. 1969. p. 86.

33. *Ibid.*, p. 86.

34. Rice. D. T., *Islamic Art*, Thames and Hudson, London. 1965. p. 183.

35. Sharif, M. M., *op. cit.*, p. 1122.

36. Hill, A., *A visual Dictionary of Art*, *op. cit.*, pp. 306 & 445.

37. Runcs, D. D., & Sichrickel, H. G., *op. cit.*, p. 486.

38. Hill, A., *op. cit.*, p. 587.

39. Bomborough, P., *op. cit.*, pp. 53-4.

40. *Ibid.*, p. 54-5.

41. *Ibid.*, p. 55.

42. Tomory, E., *op. cit.*, p. 255.

43. *Ibid.*, p. 255.

44. *Ibid.*, pp. 256-64.

CPSIA information can be obtained
at www.ICGtesting.com
Printed in the USA
LVHW021638120423
744200LV00009B/264

9 787681 902571